OUTDOOR SCULPTURE IN KALAMAZOO

FAY L. HENDRY

photography by Balthazar Korab

ιota press
Okemos, Michigan

Designed by Dorris E. Birchfield, Michigan State University

Typesetting by Superior Graphics, Lansing, Michigan

Printed by Thomson-Shore, Inc., Dexter, Michigan

Library of Congress Cataloging in Publication Data
Hendry, Fay L.   1937-
    Outdoor sculpture in Kalamazoo.
    Bibliography: p.
    Includes index.
    1. Kalamazoo, Michigan—Statues.   2. Sculpture—
Michigan—Kalamazoo.   3. Memorials—Michigan—Kalamazoo.
I. Title.
NB235.K34H46   917.74'180443   80-7501
ISBN 0-936412-01-1

FRONT COVER: Jerald W. Jackard, *The Passing of Colored Volume*
BACK COVER: Carole Harrison, detail, *Three Figures*

CONTENTS

v   Preface

vii   Acknowledgments

ix   Foreword   Eldon N. Van Liere

1   Outdoor Sculpture in Kalamazoo

13   Outdoor Sculpture by Geographic Areas

15   A. Bronson Park Area

53   B. Northeast

67   C. Southwest

95   Artists' Biographies

103   Select Bibliography

105   Index

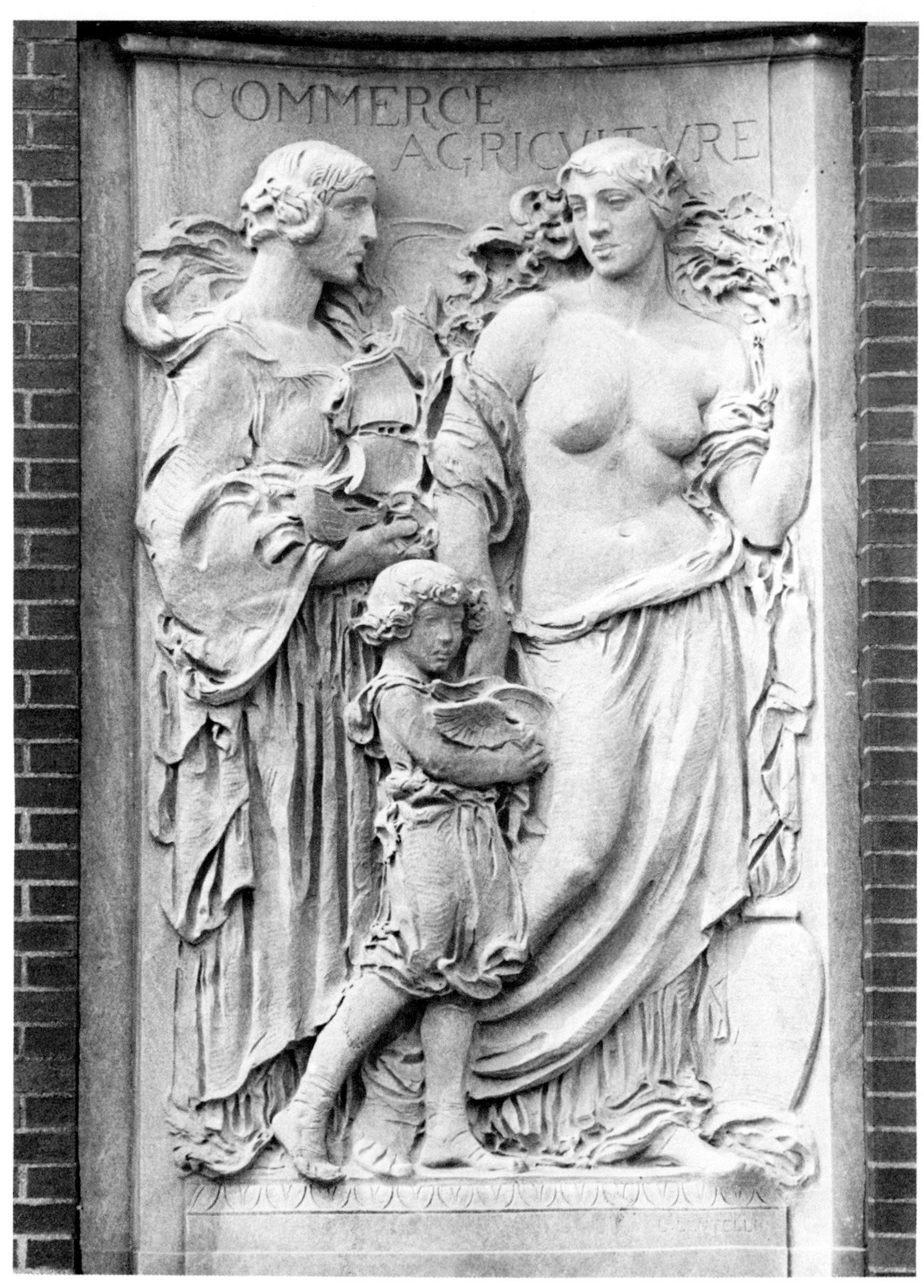

Leo Lentelli, *Commerce, Agriculture* (C-13, p. 93).

PREFACE

My interest in Michigan sculpture began in 1976 when I was hired by the Michigan History Division, Department of State, to prepare a report on cultural properties for the Coastal Zone Management Program. I intended to include information on sculpture, but when I checked possible sources, I found that practically no information was available. I was told that this wasn't New York or Washington and that there was no information because there was no sculpture.

I wondered if there were sculpture but no information, and began a study of outdoor sculpture in Lansing. Much to my surprise, there was more in the city than I or anyone else had been aware of. While much of what I recorded was not of high aesthetic merit, the sculpture yielded interesting information about the social and cultural history of Lansing. It revealed a city which neither had developed a strong sense of community identity nor had maximized its cultural potential.

The study also revealed the need to create an awareness of and appreciation for sculpture. With awareness and appreciation, there is the potential to enrich our social and cultural heritage and to influence the heritage of future generations. For sculpture not only reflects a community but contributes to it as well. It provokes sensual and intellectual responses, and it records and celebrates the human presence. It is a thread that stitches together the fabric of the past, the present, and the future.

The Lansing study led to slide presentations, tours, a television program, and a photographic exhibition, *Outdoor Sculpture in Greater Lansing: From Tombstones to Titus the Tinner,* which was held at the Michigan Historical Museum from June through December of 1977, the Society for the Study of Midwestern Literature in 1978, and the Honors College at Michigan State University in 1979. The Lansing study also led to the present expanded project, *Outdoor Sculpture in Grand Rapids, Kalamazoo, and Lansing, Michigan,* which began in 1978. Sculpture located and documented in all three cities served as the basis for the preparation of three separate guidebooks and a photographic exhibition. A public forum on outdoor sculpture will be coordinated with the exhibition which will travel to each city during 1980.

A field inventory was completed for each city of all the sculptural expressions. Free-standing, cemetery, and architectural sculpture was included regardless of aesthetic merit. A cross section of sculpture has been selected from the inventory for the guidebook with an orientation toward social and cultural history rather than aesthetic merit. Both the work of artisan and artist has been included with no intent to obscure the distinction, to disservice art, or to discourage a critical evaluation of the works.

The purpose of the guidebook is to create an awareness of outdoor sculpture in Kalamazoo and to serve as guide and an enticement to actually experience these works. For sculpture is best understood and evaluated when experienced. Entries are brief for this reason.

Entries were also limited in some cases by the constraints of time, money, and accessibility of materials. The research data which have been generated by this project will be housed in the Michigan State University Archives and Historical Collections. It is hoped that this publication will elicit further information about these works and artists. Additional information and corrections are welcomed by the author and may be sent to ιota press, 2749 E. Mt. Hope Road, Okemos, Michigan 48864.

Please note that the date for each sculpture entry refers to the time the work was created and may not necessarily refer to the date commissioned or dedicated. Dimensions refer to height and bracketed information refers to inscriptions. The biographical information for each artist, which includes additional works and their dates when available, has been accepted as given. Sculpture that is mentioned but not illustrated is indicated by a °.

Fay L. Hendry
December 21, 1979

ACKNOWLEDGMENTS

Outdoor Sculpture in Grand Rapids, Kalamazoo, and Lansing, Michigan, could not have been carried out without the help of Professor Eldon N. Van Liere, Michigan State University, and Professor Ronald Watson, Director of the Urban Institute for Contemporary Art and Chairperson of the Art Department, Aquinas College. Cooperation was also given by Fred A. Myers, former Director of the Grand Rapids Art Museum; Harry Greaver, former Director, and Thomas A. Kayser, current Director, Kalamazoo Institute of Arts; and Michael J. Smith, Chief, Michigan Historical Museum (State Museum), Lansing.

Funds for the project were provided by the Michigan State University Development Fund, the Michigan Council for the Arts, the Grand Rapids Foundation, the Kalamazoo Foundation, an anonymous Lansing donor, the Michigan Foundation for the Arts, and the Michigan Council for the Humanities.

Help has also been provided by many individuals and I apologize to anyone whose name has been omitted from the following list: Mrs. George Arend, Lyle Askew, Joseph A. Bedway, Charles E. Bennison, Mrs. George Boyce, I. W. Colburn, Nancy Donovan, Joyce Dwyer, M. D. Ellis, Robert Ewing, William P. Favorite, Martha Franklin, Roger Funk, Don M. Gury, Dave Hager, Linda Halsey, Richard Hathaway, Herbert E. Hendry, staff of the History Room, Kalamazoo Public Library, Allan Hollingsworth, Fred Honhart, Robert James, Robert Julien, F. W. Knecht, George Kooistra, Benjamin V. Lavey, Sister Mary Lawrence, Rodney Lenderink, Ray Mackie, David McShane, Catherine Madsen, Larry Massie, Charles Meyer, Patricia Gordon Michael, Cindy Newman, Sesta Peekstok, Darlene Pontello, Alexis Praus, Ray Purdin, Rose Reimveld, Dan Ryan, Ilene Schechter, Peter Schmitt,

Helen Sheridan, Webster Smith, Craig Staudenbaur, Marjorie Staudenbaur, Mary Lou Stewart, Shirlee Studt, Richard E. Sullivan, James J. Thompson, James Vermeulen, Linda Wagner, Leon E. Wallace, Sister Catherine Ward, Velma G. Wilson, Mrs. Lloyd Yenner, and Deborah Zelinger. I am, of course, indebted to all the artists both living and dead who are the substance of this project.

FOREWORD

The public sculpture, researched and catalogued almost single-handedly by Fay Hendry and masterfully photographed by Balthazar Korab, presented in this guide documents the works in this community which have survived from the past and those which are being created today. The old sculptures are familiar for they have been around a long time, but they have become remote in meaning, and much of the most modern of sculpture seems remote by design. Public sculpture has never had an easy time of it, for it is asked to do the impossible—to please a wide diversity of tastes and interests. The very fact that it is public and thereby unavoidable tends to make it controversial.

In the past public sculpture, whether it served to decorate a building or was a freestanding work, served very clear humanizing purposes. More often than not the intent was didactic, and when it was not, as in the case of an ornamental carving, its purpose was to give the eye a moment of delight. Modern taste has done much to obscure these monuments from the past with the exception of those sacred precincts where we have buried the past and collected monuments to the dead. Beyond these hallowed grounds the market place takes over, and the monuments that dominate are huge impersonal buildings of a democratic sameness lacking, or nearly so, that humanizing touch of decorative sculpture. The older buildings which survive and do have some sculpture adorning them seem either quaint or too unique to exist comfortably with the shivering towers of steel and glass that surround them. It is as if these reminders of past individualism are threats to a predominant concept of equality and sameness.

If modern architecture has left little room for the decorative or allegorical relief on its surfaces, it has completely dwarfed the freestanding sculpture both old and new. To be sure, man has been made puny by much of modern architecture, but we for the most part accommodate ourselves to it; however, should that urban pedestrian look up and take note of some sculpture dwarfed by monuments to commerce and politics, he or she might be struck by how scale and

space have changed in the twentieth century. The old sculpture may
have been preserved, but very often its setting has not, and the
sculpture comes out the loser. Much of modern sculpture has adopted
an industrial tone with its use of polished chrome-like surfaces or
sheet steel, rusted or painted, welded or bolted together allowing for a
scale that can attempt to compete with huge buildings in a
vernacular common with them and be eye-catching in the midst
of an urban bustle.

Modern sculpture with its concerns for pure form has the potential
of universality. Pure form can be understood by all and/or be moving
to all; but, despite this potential, it is, nevertheless, found
incomprehensible by many. Pure form does not read like a bronze
figure of a dancing young woman draped in garlands of flowers
representing Spring. To the viewer with an eye for pure form the very
pose of such a figure with its tensions and balances may be most
satisfying, but the allegorical aspect is a distraction. On the other hand,
the message of Spring's celebration of a liberation from winter and the
hope for the fertile months ahead as well as a comprehensible technical
skill at rendering a likeness are understandable to all. Thus, there is in
the dancing maiden a community comprehension on a multitude of
levels denied by many modern works despite their "universality."
Sculpture free of representation and allegory in search of purity can be
and has come to be appreciated or accepted by many, but it does not
serve to reinforce any vision of public values other than the belief that
art has a place in public life and in some general way is uplifting and
enriching.

This guidebook is an attempt to help us all pause as we hurry by and
take note of how one generation sought to speak to another without
asking us to go into a museum or pore over a book. The illustrations
herein isolate the sculpture as much as possible from the competing and
often overwhelming surrounding distractions to help direct our eyes to
what we have here and perhaps inspire us to make public sculpture a
meaningful expression of our own time.

Eldon N. Van Liere

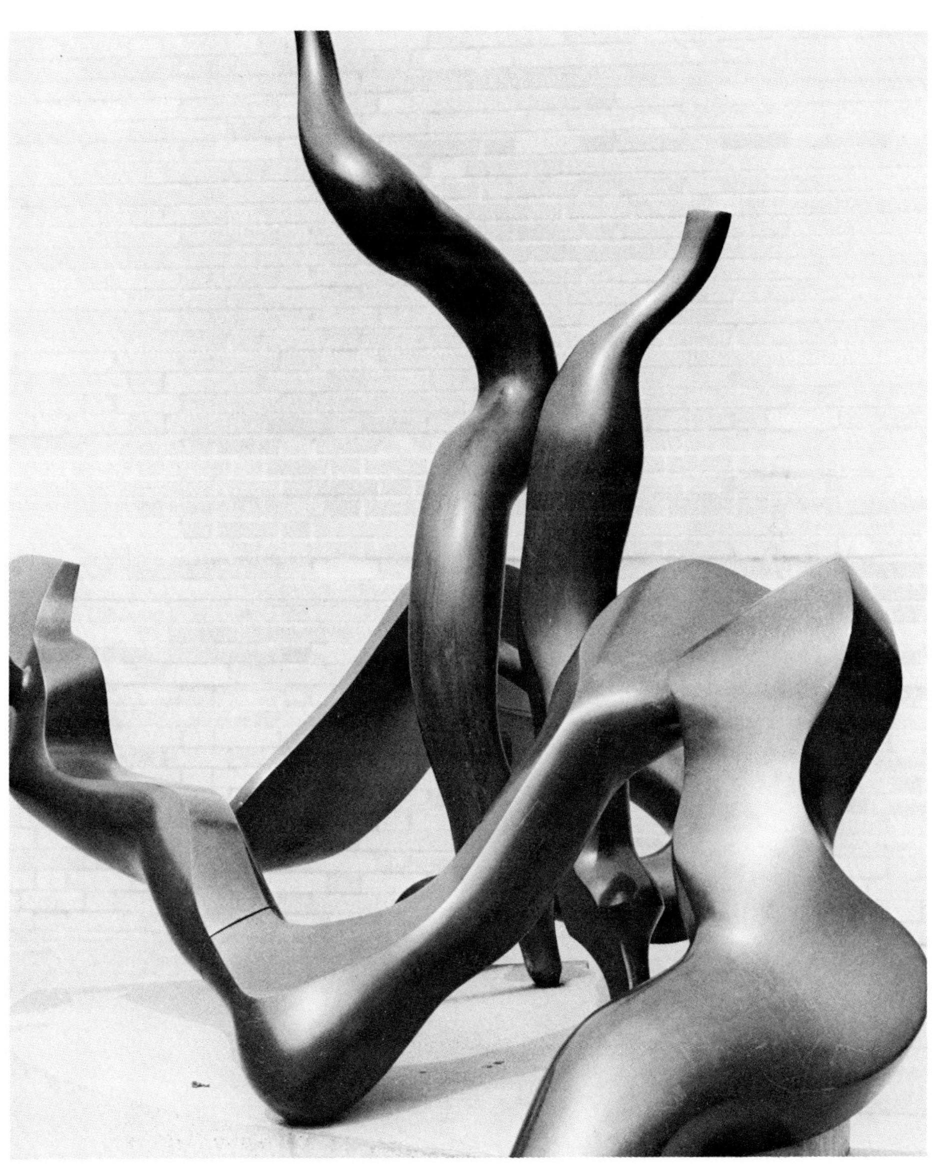

Detail: Dwayne Lowder, Untitled (A-6, p. 27).

OUTDOOR SCULPTURE IN KALAMAZOO

By the 1830s Michigan was ripe for statehood. The fur trade was peaking, the Indians had ceded most of their lands, and transportation was greatly facilitated by the construction of arteries like the Erie Canal, the Old Sauk Trail (US 12), and the Territorial Road (I-94). The latter passed through Kalamazoo, connecting Detroit with St. Joseph and ultimately with Chicago. Land speculators and settlers, primarily from New England and New York, began streaming into the territory.

By the time Michigan achieved statehood in 1837, Kalamazoo was one of the thriving settlements along the Territorial Road. The first settler, Titus Bronson, camped on the present site of Bronson Park in 1829. The colorful Bronson and his brother-in-law, Stephen H. Richardson, platted the Village of Bronson on March 12, 1831. Bronson's generous offer to provide land in the center of the village for a courthouse, jail, academy, churches, schools, and a burial ground, probably resulted in the location of the county seat at Bronson on January 15, 1831. On April 1, 1836, the name of the village was officially changed to the Indian name of Kalamazoo. Bronson, distressed by the name change, as the story goes, left Kalamazoo to live in several other settlements, just as he had done before coming to Kalamazoo.

The name Kalamazoo, which literally means "boiling pot," had also been given to the river flowing through the city, and to the county. The word may refer to the eddies in the Kalamazoo River, the mists rising from the river, or races which were run between the river and some point and which had to be completed before a pot began to boil or before a pot boiled dry.

Though a trading post was located on the Kalamazoo River near the present location of Riverview Cemetery, the heart of Kalamazoo has remained where Bronson first established it. In 1854, the county leased the two village squares to the Village of Kalamazoo to be used as a park. At that time Bronson Park, which did not receive its official name until December 6, 1876, was divided by Church Street with the jail and an Indian mound located on the western half and the Academy on the eastern side. In addition to having an Indian mound, the park is also the only site in Michigan where Abraham Lincoln delivered a speech. That auspicious day was August 27, 1856.

After the city took over the park in 1854, the two squares were unified by closing off Church Street and in 1857 the last of the two buildings, the Academy, originally a branch of the University of Michigan, was removed. In 1878, a park design by Adam Oliver was completed. Samuel W. Durant, author of the *History of Kalamazoo County, Michigan* (1880), describes the newly designed park in the following manner:

> . . .a large amount of labor and money have been expended in beautifying the park, and it is now all that the most fastidious taste could desire. The fence has been entirely removed, the ground carefully leveled and smoothed, fine broad walks constructed, a magnificent fountain erected, trees planted, and everything made as perfect as possible, and there could be no finer or more agreeable spot found in which to spend an hour in the opening days of spring or on a sweltering August afternoon. Many of the old "burr-oaks" of primeval growth have been preserved, and a large number of maple and other trees planted.
>
> This elegant park is surrounded by fine public buildings, including three churches and the new county prison, and many costly and tastefully-arranged dwellings and lawns, and when a solid gravel walk shall be completed around its margin, but little additional expense will be required to keep it in fine condition (p. 270).

The nineteenth-century fountain was replaced by the McColl Memorial Fountain in 1927, but objections to that "siloesque" fountain soon led to its replacement with Alfonso Iannelli's *Fountain of the Pioneers* (1939) [p. 17]. In 1976, Kirk Newman's Bicentennial fountain, *When Justice and Mercy Prevail, Children May Safely Play* (1976) [p. 18], was placed at the opposite end of the park. Also located in the park, in addition to several markers, are Charles Keck's U.S.S. *Maine* Memorial Tablet (1913) [p. 20] and *The Hiker* by Theodore Alice Ruggles Kitson (c. 1923) [p. 22].

The tradition of encircling the square with civic buildings continues today. The present City Hall, located south of the park, carries reliefs by the Studio of Architectural Sculpture (1931) [p. 39]. The reliefs and the Cathedral Church of Christ the King located on I-94. They serve as a reminder of Kalamazoo's location on the old Territorial Road which played a role in the development of the state and the Midwest. Other examples of decorative sculpture include the two classical women and other reliefs by an unknown artist on the Kalamazoo Gazette Building (c. 1925) [p. 45], and the weathervane of a "Boy Reading a Book," also by an unknown artist, on the Washington Square Library (c. 1927) [p. 88]. High cost and the preference for streamlined modern architecture during the depression sounded the death knell for decorative terra cotta and lead to the decline of sculptural decoration in general. A curious mix can be found on the City Hall with its forward-looking, streamlined silhouette and decorative elements which look back to the nineteenth century.

The seminal modern art movement had already begun to challenge the flourishing Beaux-Arts school at the beginning of the twentieth century. Artists began to carve directly in wood and stone. Since they responded to the natural forms of the material, their works tended toward abstraction. The stone carver was thus eliminated and works became smaller and more intimate. A new class of patrons was beginning to develop which could afford sculpture for private settings, though their tastes continued to embrace traditional styles rather than modern art. Garden sculpture, funerary memorials, and copies of classical works like the Luca della Robbia reliefs on the Zelinger House (c. 1910) [p. 87] were popular.

Between World War I and World War II, a new style developed which was more in keeping with the twentieth century. Once again, the style originated in Paris and was called Art Moderne or Art Deco after the 1925 Exhibition of Decorative and Industrial Arts. This crisp, geometric style created a streamlined yet bold effect which is reflected in the Iannelli *Fountain of the Pioneers* cited above. A softer Art Deco can be found in Corrado Joseph Parducci's *Justice, Vigilance, Law,* and other reliefs located on the Kalamazoo County Building or the reliefs by an unknown artist on the Henry Vandercook Hall for Men (1939)° and the Lavinia Spindler Hall for Women (1940) [p. 76] located at Western Michigan University. Art Deco, particularly as a figurative style, continued on through the 1950s in a progressively bland manner. These

supermuscled heroes represented American ideals until an abstract
vocabulary received public support and acceptance in the 1960s.

The 1930s depression provided an impetus for the proliferation of
these bulky, angular figures. During this period of social concern, there
was an inward turning and an emphasis on the individual worker. The
United States government emerged as a patron of the arts through
programs like the Works Progress Administration (WPA), Federal Art
Project. Initiated in 1935, the name of the program was changed to the
Work Projects Administration in 1939 and was terminated in 1942. The
sculptural reliefs for the dormitories at Western Michigan University
were created through the WPA. Though the sculptural reliefs for the
Kalamazoo County Building reflect a thirties figural style and the
building itself was constructed through another New Deal program, the
Public Works Administration (PWA), according to the sculptor Parducci,
the reliefs were not created through any Federal relief program.

For the most part, it appears that Kalamazoo did not participate to
any great extent in WPA sculptural projects. In fact, there was very
little sculptural activity between 1940 and 1960 in Kalamazoo. One
exception is Bernhard Zuckermann's *Waders* (1935) [p. 90] which was
placed in Mount Ever-Rest Memorial Park in 1955. Between 1960 and
1970 he also carved four marble sculptures for that cemetery. °

It was not until after World War II that modern sculpture began to
blossom, even though the seeds had been sown and cultivated
throughout the first half of the twentieth century. Traditional form
(often the human form) and space were in the process of
transformation through new materials, techniques, and thought.
Representational forms were abstracted into organic and geometric
forms. The relationship of space to a solid mass was altered by
incorporating space within the form. As pedestals began to disappear,
space was increasingly extended and the viewer was increasingly
involved with the work. Such spatial transformations have paved the
way for today's large-scale works which embrace a total environment.

The application of industrial materials like steel and plastic and
industrial techniques like welding allowed sculpture to be constructed
rather than modeled or carved. Sculpture could incorporate found
objects or have movable parts. Sculptors were no longer bound to

express heroic American ideals in their work but were free to explore sculpture as an individual expression. Today, the subject of sculpture may be form, materials, process, or something as ephemeral as a concept or performace. The dimensions of sculpture can be stretched even further if one includes permanent works like photographs or video tapes which document ephemeral art.

Kalamazoo's first abstract work was Kirk Newman's fountain (1959)° which was commissioned by the city of Kalamazoo for the first pedestrian mall ever to be constructed in the United States. A mixed response to the content and uninvited misting of pedestrians eventually led to the removal of the fountain when the mall was renovated in 1971. The fountain was moved to Bronson Park and was later destroyed at the request of the artist when his new fountain, *When Justice and Mercy Prevail, Children May Safely Play,* was installed there in 1976. Also located in the mall is Douglas Gruizenga's *Industrial Forms II* (1974-1975) [p. 50] and the Seth Thomas Clock.

During the 1960s Urban Renewal programs, which sometimes included similar mall projects, were initiated across the United States in an attempt to revitalize decaying inner cities. Old structures were razed to make way for the new. Once again the government became and continues to be a patron of the arts through programs like Urban Renewal, the National Endowment for the Arts, the General Services Art-in-Architecture Program, and the Michigan Council for the Arts. It would appear, however, that there is no sculpture in Kalamazoo which can be directly related to any of these programs.

In addition to the city and Nazareth College, there are other cultural pockets which also contain sculpture. Located at the Kalamazoo Institute of Arts are Jerald Jackard's *Passing of Colored Volume* (1968) [p. 33]; Carole Harrison's *Seated Female* (1969) [p. 28]; Dwayne Lowder's untitled sculpture (1969) [p. 27]; Kirk Newman's *People;* and George Rickey's *Four Lines Oblique Gyratory, Variation IV* (1973) [p. 31]. Bernard Palchick's *Détente* (1973) [p. 72] can be found at Kalamazoo College, a Baptist-affiliated school which was founded in 1833. Western Michigan University, originally Western State Normal School, has recently added sculpture to its campus, primarily through the efforts of Professor Charles Myer, faculty member and former chairperson of the art department. These sculptures include Gerald Dumlao's *Sun Disc* (1971) [p. 82]; Carole Harrison's *Three Figures* (1971) [p. 80]; and Douglas Gruizenga's untitled work (1972) [p. 78].

In 1978, the Kalamazoo Arts Council commissioned *Road Piece*° from James Chressanthis for its arts festival, Super Summer. The work was located on city property alongside the railroad tracks outside of the new Intermodal Transportaion Center. The piece was removed in 1979 because of negative reactions from the community.

It is this broad mix of conservative and progressive elements which has marked the sculptural heritage of Kalamazoo. Patronage ranges from the arts community to the general public who contributed to the Bicentennial fountain, *When Justice and Mercy Prevail, Children May Safely Play.* It also includes wealthy patrons like Mrs. Dorothy Upjohn Dalton, who is associated with the well-known pharmaceutical firm the Upjohn Company. Her generous cultural contributions include monies for the following sculptures which were mentioned above: Carole Harrison's *Seated Female,* Dwayne Lowder's untitled work, and Kirk Newman's *People,* all located at the Kalamazoo Institute of Art, and Carole Harrison's *Three Figures* located at Western Michigan University.

Kalamazoo is also known for its paper industry and as the site of the Kalamazoo State Hospital, formerly the Michigan Asylum for the Insane. In the past Kalamazoo was known for its production of stoves and cultivation of celery. None of these aspects of Kalamazoo is directly reflected in sculpture except for the sculptural decoration on the quadrangle of buildings surrounding the unusual water tower at the Kalamazoo State Hospital. The buildings were designed by Knecht, McCarty and Thebaud of Grand Rapids around 1940. According to F. W. Knecht, some of the heads which appear above the doorways° represent former medical directors of that institution.

Because Kalamazoo is so well-rooted and diverse, it is difficult to predict what the sculptural activity of this selective and individualized city will hold for the 1980s. The least that one can say is that it will be interesting. For, it appears to be true one hundred years after Durant made his statement that Kalamazoo still has "all the habiliments of a modern city, except the name and those extravagances which too often accompany titles of nobility."

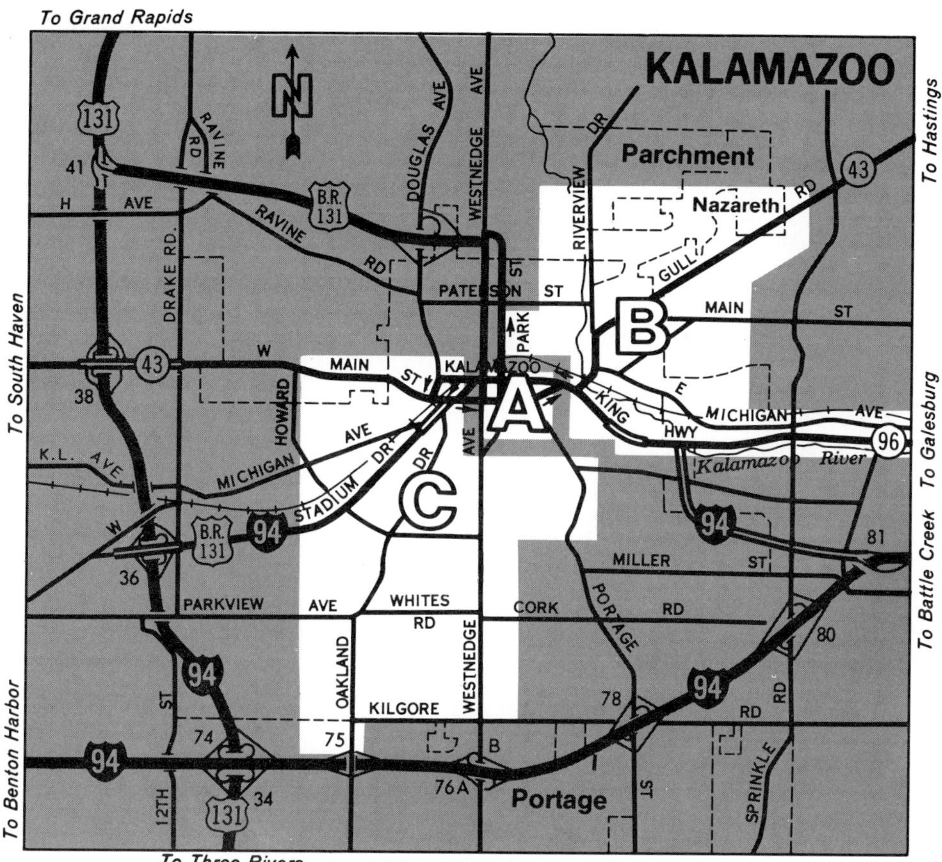

OUTDOOR SCULPTURE
BY GEOGRAPHIC AREAS

A. BRONSON PARK AREA

B. NORTHEAST

C. SOUTHWEST

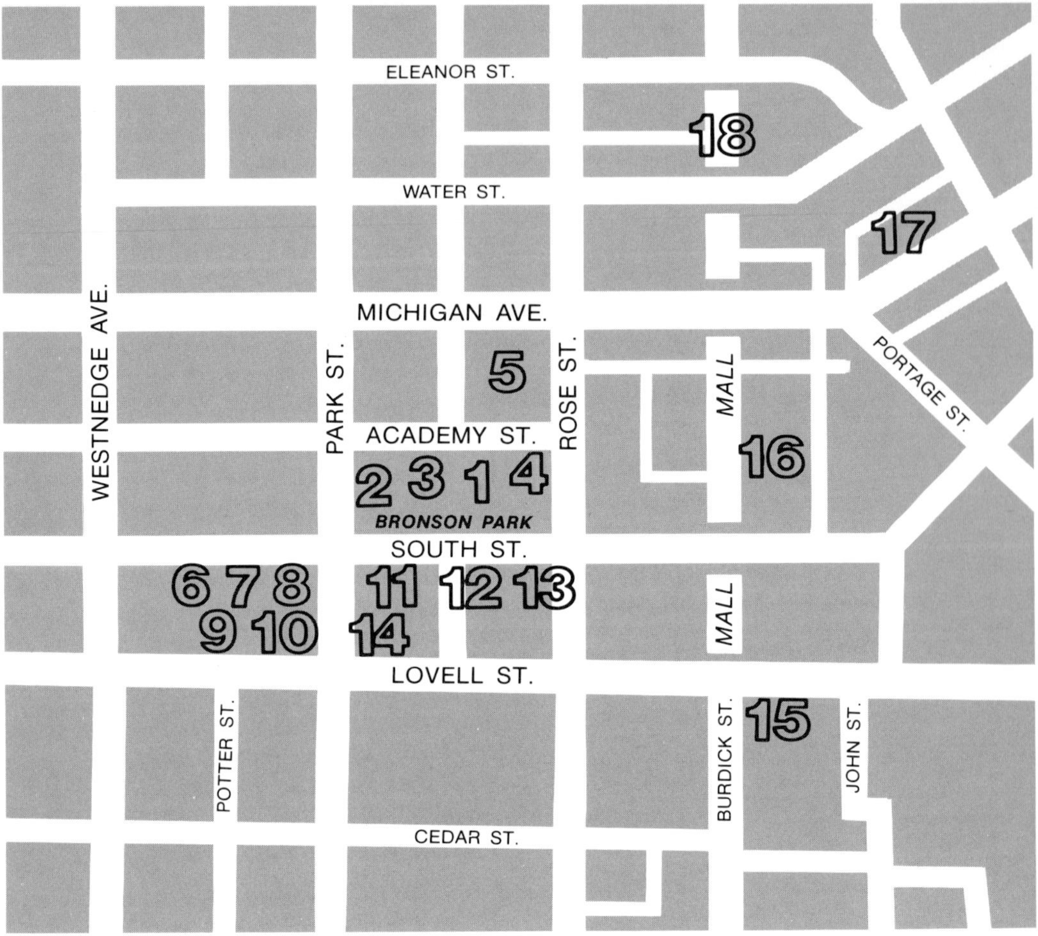

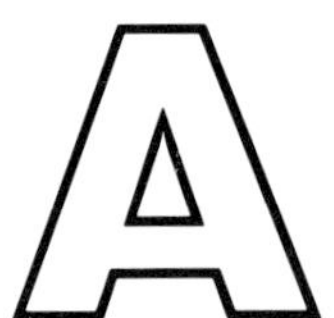

A

BRONSON PARK AREA

1. Alfonso Iannelli, FOUNTAIN OF THE PIONEERS
   Bronson Park

2. Kirk Newman, WHEN JUSTICE AND MERCY PREVAIL,...
   Bronson Park

3. Charles Keck, U.S.S. MAINE MEMORIAL TABLET
   Bronson Park

4. Theodore Alice Ruggles Kitson, THE HIKER
   Bronson Park

5. Corrado Joseph Parducci, KALAMAZOO COUNTY BUILDING RELIEFS
   Kalamazoo County Building

6. Dwayne Lowder, UNTITLED
   Kalamazoo Institute of Arts

7. Carole Harrison, SEATED FEMALE
   Kalamazoo Institute of Arts

8. George Rickey, FOUR LINES OBLIQUE GYRATORY, VARIATION IV
   Kalamazoo Institute of Arts

9. Jerald W. Jackard (Jacquard), THE PASSING OF COLORED VOLUME
   Kalamazoo Institute of Arts

10. Kirk Newman, PEOPLE
    Kalamazoo Institute of Arts

11. Alois Lang (?), ANGEL
    First Presbyterian Church

12. Studio of Architectural Sculpture, CITY HALL RELIEFS
    City Hall

13. Artist Unknown, PARK CLUB DOOR RELIEFS
    Park Club

14. Artist Unknown (replica Leon E. Wallace), GARGOYLE
    Ladies Library Association

15. Artist Unknown, KALAMAZOO GAZETTE BUILDING RELIEFS
    Kalamazoo Gazette Building

16. Artist Unknown, SETH THOMAS CLOCK
    Mackie and Ellis Jewelers

17. Artist Unknown, SCHAU-POWELL SPORT CENTRE RELIEFS
    Schau-Powell Sport Centre

18. Douglas M. Gruizenga, INDUSTRIAL FORMS II
    North Kalamazoo Mall

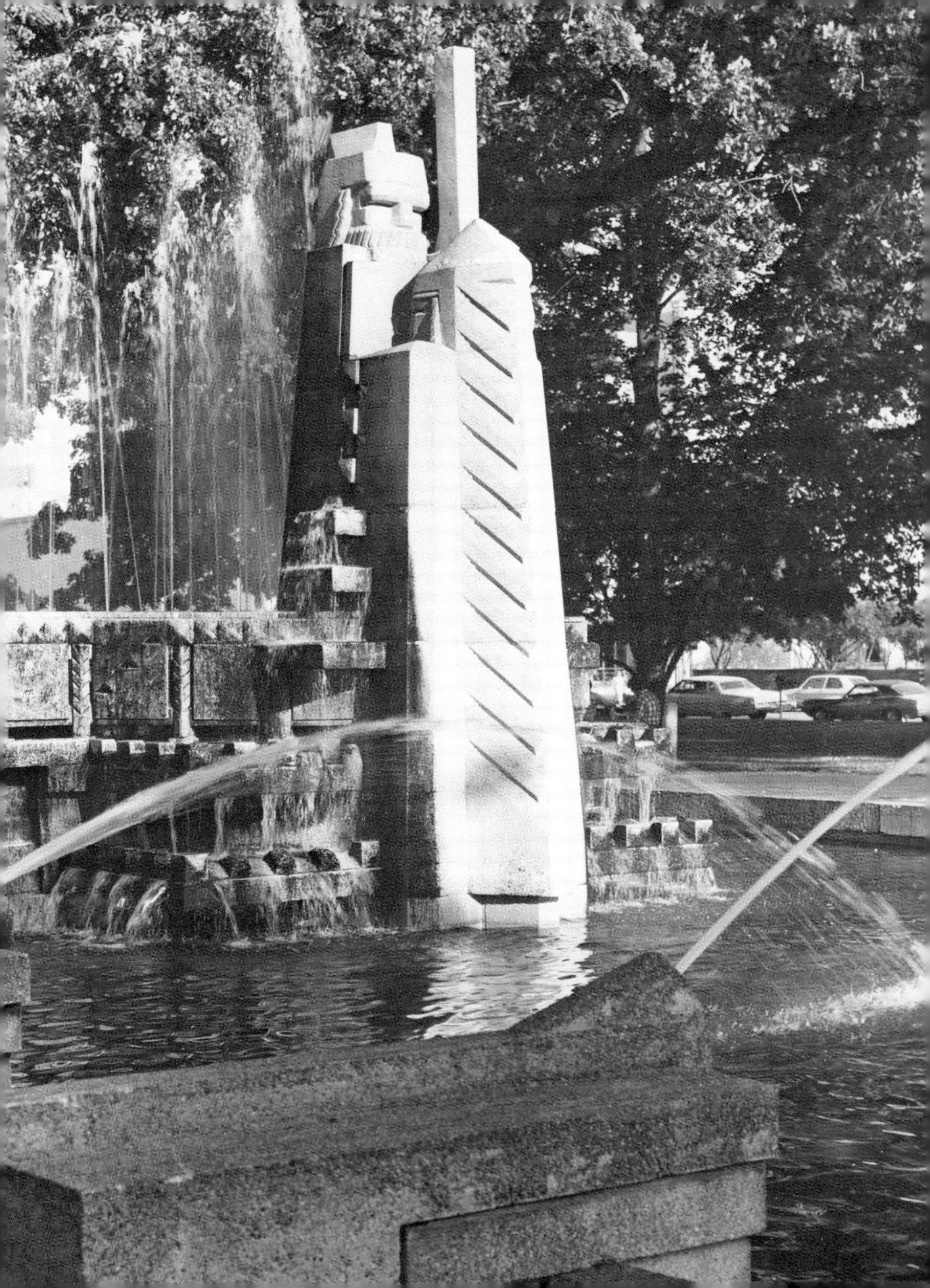

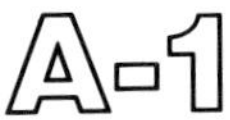

Alfonso Iannelli (1888-1965)

FOUNTAIN OF THE PIONEERS

1939, concrete, c. 19'

Bronson Park
Park, South, Rose, and Academy streets, Kalamazoo

The fourth and present fountain in Bronson Park grew out of a desire to replace the "siloesque" electric McColl Memorial Fountain which was erected in 1927. The Business and Professional Women's Club held a nationwide contest in 1936 and the winner was Marcelline Gougler, former pupil of Alfonso Iannelli. Iannelli, who had advised Gougler on her designs, was called in as a consultant and eventually developed the final design. Funds for the fountain were provided through the Works Progress Administration and the fountain was dedicated on June 6, 1940. The influence of Frank Lloyd Wright (1869-1959), with whom Iannelli had worked on the since-demolished Midway Gardens in Chicago, can be felt in this angular low-lying fountain which employs the chevron and other geometric Art Deco motifs. The fountain reads like a history book, as does Bronson Park, which was named after Titus Bronson. Bronson, who also gave his name to the town, later renamed Kalamazoo, first camped on the site of an Indian mound which later became the public square and focal point of the city. The fountain, oriented toward the west, portrays an armed white man towering over and absorbing a dignified Indian. The decorative motifs around the walls of the fountain and the movement of the water suggest the rich fertility of the area. The fountain was never completed; a glass panel was intended to project from the pioneer's head to symbolize his vision and a glass and metal panel, connecting the pioneer to the center of the fountain, was intended to symbolize industrial progress.

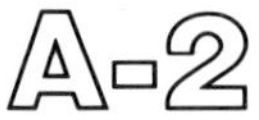

Kirk Newman (1926-   )

WHEN JUSTICE AND MERCY PREVAIL, CHILDREN MAY SAFELY PLAY

1976, bronze, lifesize figures

Bronson Park
Park, South, Rose, and Academy streets, Kalamazoo

The fountain sculpture was commissioned by the religious communities of Kalamazoo to celebrate America's Bicentennial. Funds were collected from groups and individuals and the work was dedicated on July 4, 1976. The group desired an immediately recognizable work, and after considering sculpture proposals from artists throughout the United States, they selected Kalamazoo artist Kirk Newman to create a work consisting of nine children and a prophet figure. Kalamazoo children of various age, religious, and ethnic groups served as models. Because children are fresh and can be shaped, they represent hope for the future. A stele containing an emerging, fragmented prophet figure represents the past and the present. The prophet figure serves as a reminder that mankind, who unintentionally prophesys his own future, continually comes from the earth and disappears. It is while human beings are on earth that they have the opportunity to create "towns without walls" as urged by the prophet Zechariah in the sixth century B.C. "And the streets of the city shall be full of boys and girls playing in the streets thereof." (Zechariah 8:5)

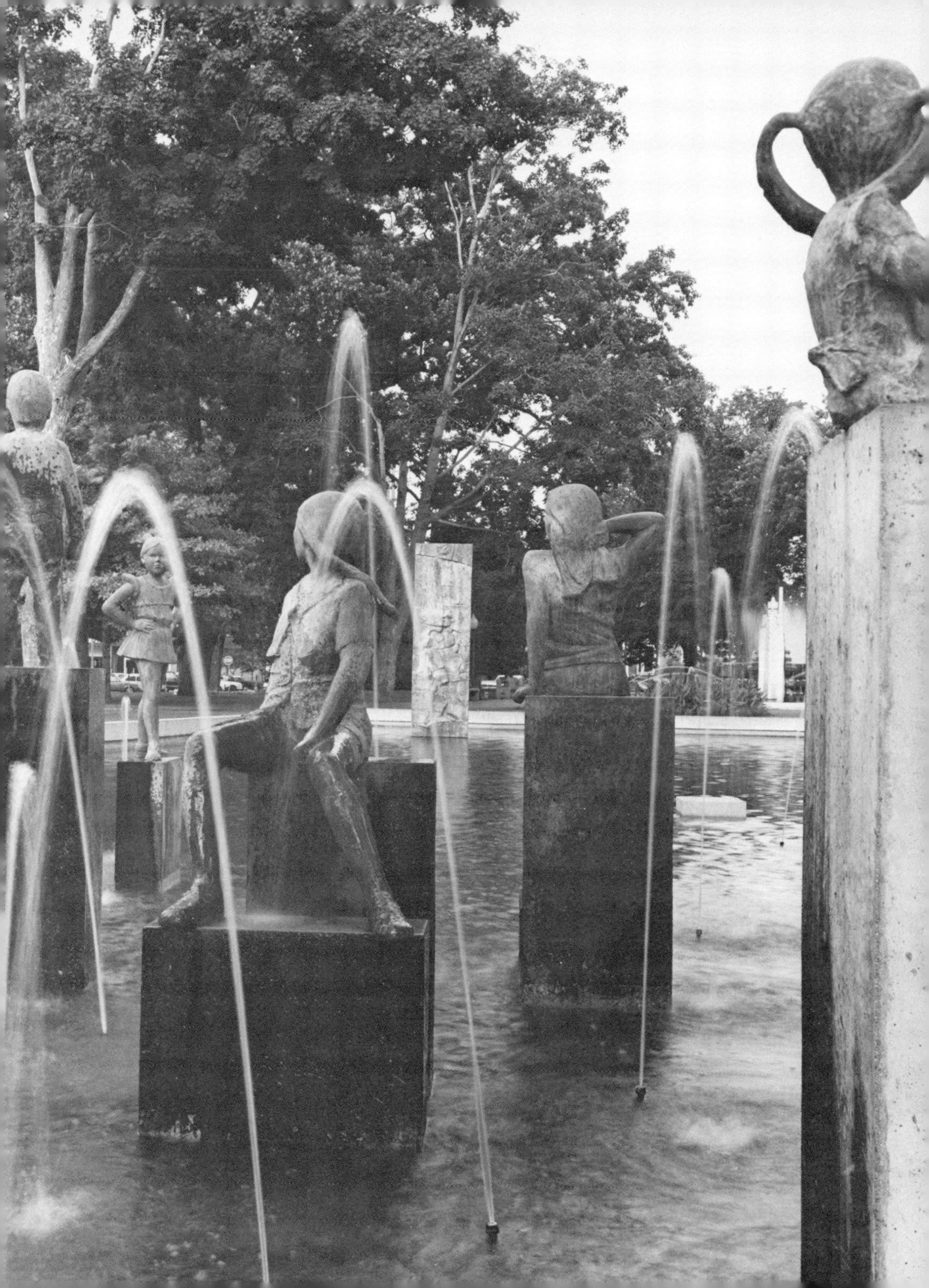

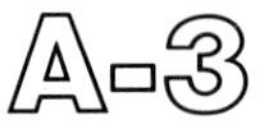

Charles Keck (1874-1951)
U.S.S. MAINE MEMORIAL TABLET

1913, bronze, 13"
[© C. Keck Sc   1913   Cast by Jno. Williams Inc.   N.Y.   #336]

Bronson Park
Park, South, Rose, and Academy streets, Kalamazoo

On February 15, 1898, the U.S.S. *Maine* exploded in the harbor of Havana, Cuba. Although never proved to be sabotage, this event was a major cause of the Spanish American War; it also initiated the battle cry "Remember the *Maine*." For fourteen years the partially submerged *Maine* lay in the harbor until it was raised and reburied in 1912. When the United States Government announced that the ship would be salvaged, requests for relics were received. Because there were not enough suitable relics, one thousand memorial tablets were cast from equipment and parts of the wreck. The Commission of Fine Arts advised the Navy and War Departments on the preparation of the tablets which were distributed to veterans and other groups. The Kalamazoo tablet was requested by the Orcutt Post No. 79, Grand Army of the Republic, on behalf of the Richard Westnedge Camp No. 16, United States Spanish War Veterans and dedicated on November 19, 1913. The memorial tablet portrays a classical mourning figure, variously called Liberty, Columbia, or Victory, extending her right arm toward the palm branch of victory while holding a shield with the arms of the United States in her left arm. In the background lies the sunken *Maine*. Another casting of the tablet is located below *General William Rufus Shafter* in nearby Galesburg (see p. 65).

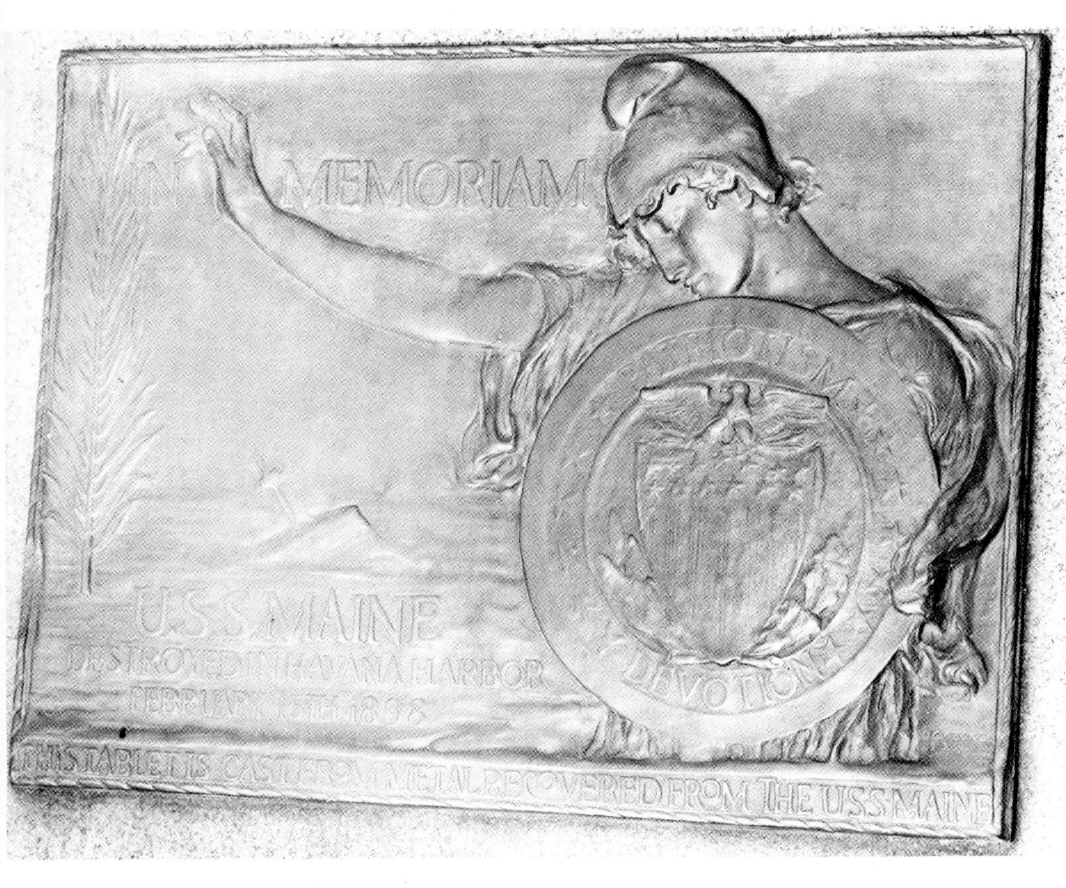
IN MEMORIAM
PATRIOTISM
DEVOTION
U.S.S. MAINE
DESTROYED IN HAVANA HARBOR
FEBRUARY 15TH 1898
THIS TABLET IS CAST FROM METAL RECOVERED FROM THE U.S.S. MAINE

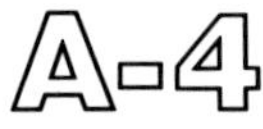

Theodore Alice Ruggles Kitson (1871-1932)
THE HIKER

c. 1923, bronze, 8'5"
[Theo. A. R. Kitson Sc   Gorham Co. Founders]

Bronson Park
Park, South, Rose, and Academy streets, Kalamazoo

The hiker, so called because of his long hikes in the hot
steaming jungles, fought in the name of freedom, humanity,
and patriotism in Cuba and the Philippine Islands and in a relief
expedition to China during the Boxer Rebellion. The
romanticized treatment of this foot soldier suggests the
popularity of "this splendid little war," the Spanish American
War of 1898-1902, in which the United States emerged as a
world power and expanded its territories to include Puerto
Rico, Guam, and the Philippine Islands. The monument was
erected by the citizens of Kalamazoo city and county under the
auspices of the Richard Westnedge Camp No. 16, United
Spanish War Veterans. The dedication was the opening
ceremony for the observance of Memorial Day on May 30,
1924. Approximately fifty other castings of *The Hiker* can be
found in cities throughout the United States, including the
original which was erected at the University of Minnesota in
1906. Two others can be found in the Michigan cities of
Grand Rapids (c. 1927) and Lansing (c. 1945).

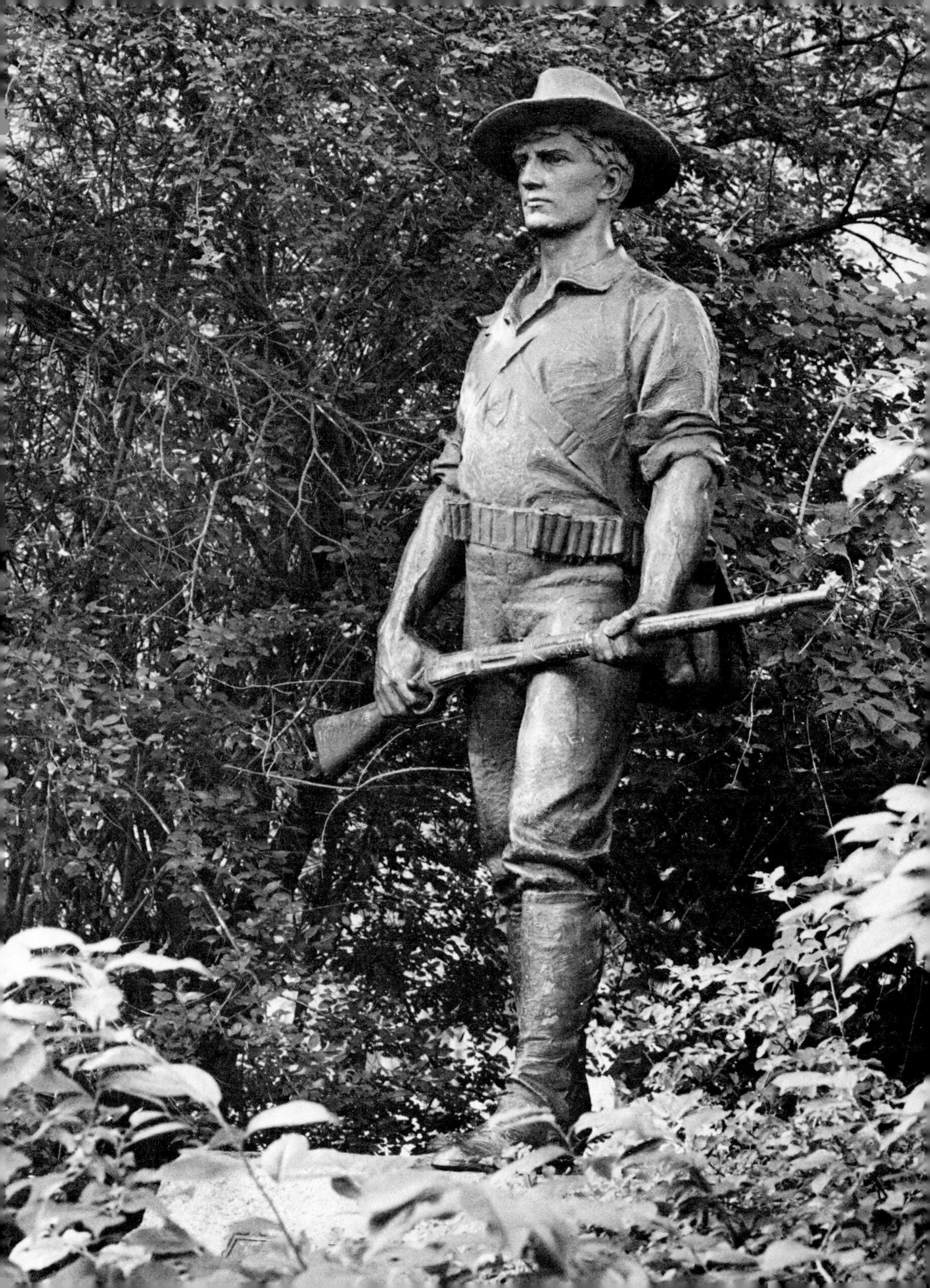

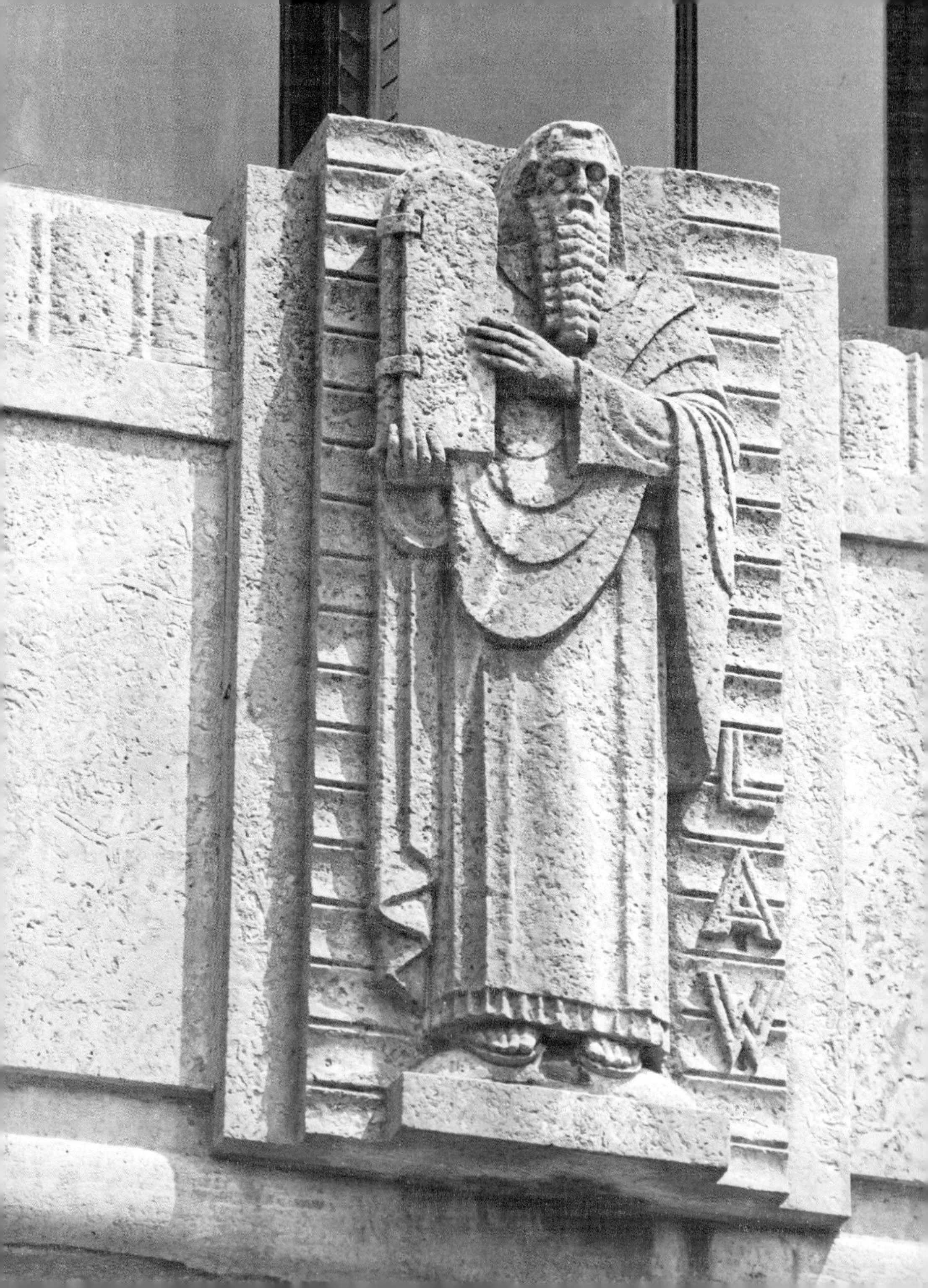
L
A
W

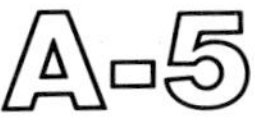

KALAMAZOO COUNTY BUILDING RELIEFS

1936-1937, Mankato stone, LAW c. 5'

Kalamazoo County Building
227 W. Michigan Avenue, Kalamazoo

The present Art Deco County Building was dedicated on October 16, 1937. It occupies the site of the first County Building which was erected one hundred years earlier on property owned by the founder of the city, Titus Bronson. The building was designed by Kalamazoo architect M. J. C. Billingham (1885-1959) with Smith, Hinchman & Grylls of Detroit as associate architects. Constructed during the depression through the Public Works Administration (PWA), it provided much-needed office space and a new jail. Located on the north and south facades of the building are allegorical figures of *Justice, Law,* and *Vigilance.* Originally there were bronze doors beneath the central figure of *Law* which contained additional figures alluding to the arts of civilization. The doors, removed in 1979, portray *Industry, Education, Commerce, Law, Science,* and *Agriculture.*

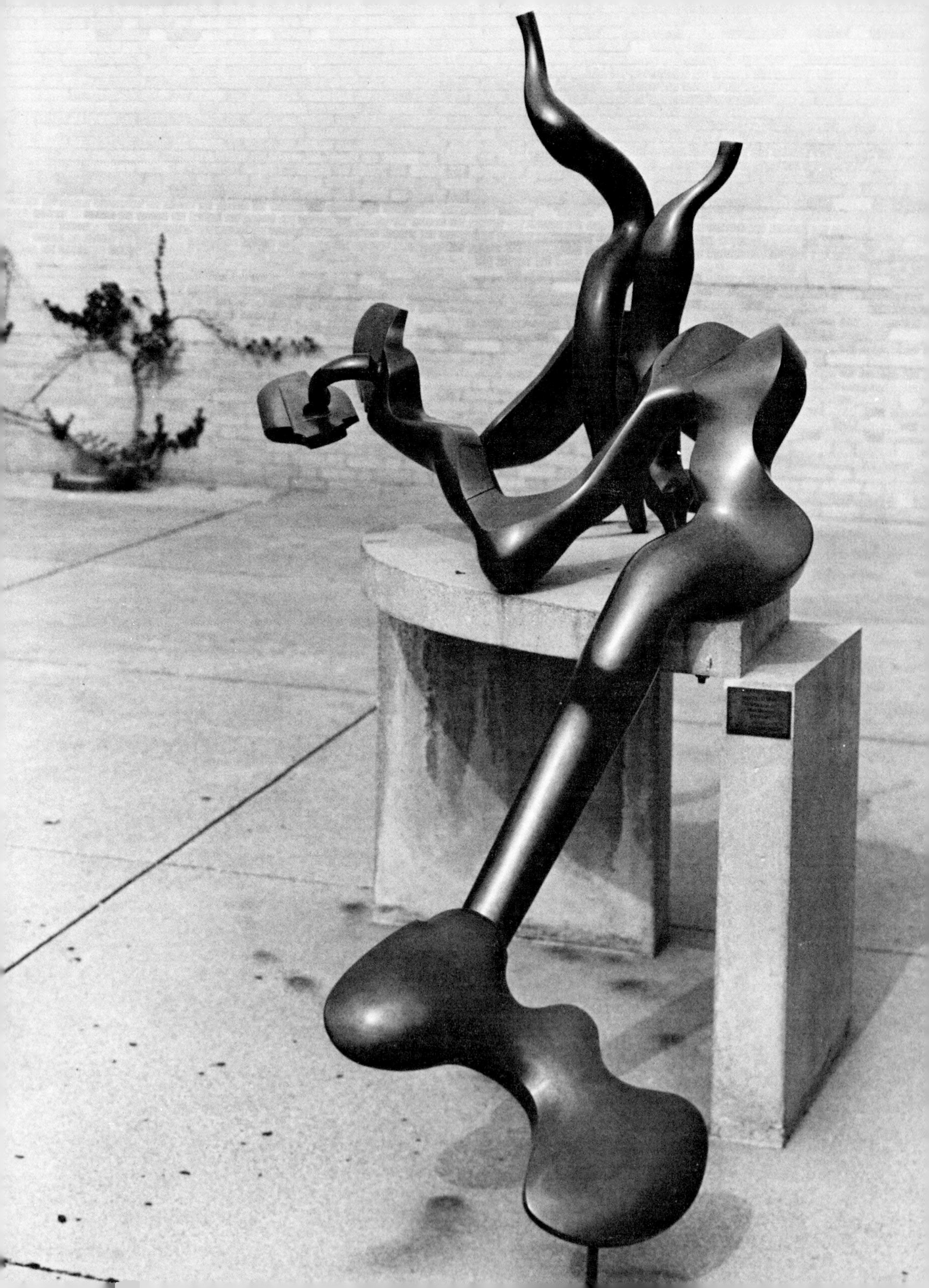

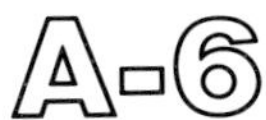

Dwayne Lowder (1936-   )
UNTITLED

1969, bronze, 6'3"

Kalamazoo Institute of Arts
314 S. Park Street, Kalamazoo

This sculpture and a piece by Carole Harrison were commissioned for the courtyard of the Kalamazoo Institute of Arts. Funds were provided by Mrs. Dorothy Upjohn Dalton and the works were unveiled on January 28, 1970. Dwayne Lowder, who had never accepted a commission previously, developed the piece out of a pair of wooden sculptures titled *Apollo* and *Cadmus.* Both works are composed of organic surrealistic forms which reflect the story of Cadmus and Lowder's interest in dream imagery. Apollo had forecast in a dream that Cadmus would become king. The reclining figure of Cadmus, founder of Thebes, is the basis of the present untitled sculpture. The piece was originally a shiny bronze with metallic orange and green planar surfaces which defined the shifts and nuances of the sinuous forms. Because of oxidation, the sculpture was repatined in black; now light and shadow perform the previous function of the color.

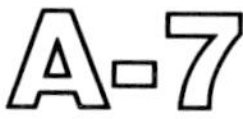

Carole Harrison (1933-   )
SEATED FEMALE

1969, brass, 7'4"

Kalamazoo Institute of Arts
314 S. Park Street, Kalamazoo

Seated Female was commissioned by the Kalamazoo
Institute of Arts with funds provided by Mrs. Dorothy
Upjohn Dalton and was unveiled on January 28, 1970.
The piece explores the inner psyche of women and
reflects Carole Harrison's interest in the women's
movement at that time. The cast brass segments,
accentuated by textured junctures, form a complex
juxtaposition of fluid and harsh shapes and lines. The
figure suggests the complexity and wide range of human
emotions which may be boxed in or allowed to flow
spontaneously.

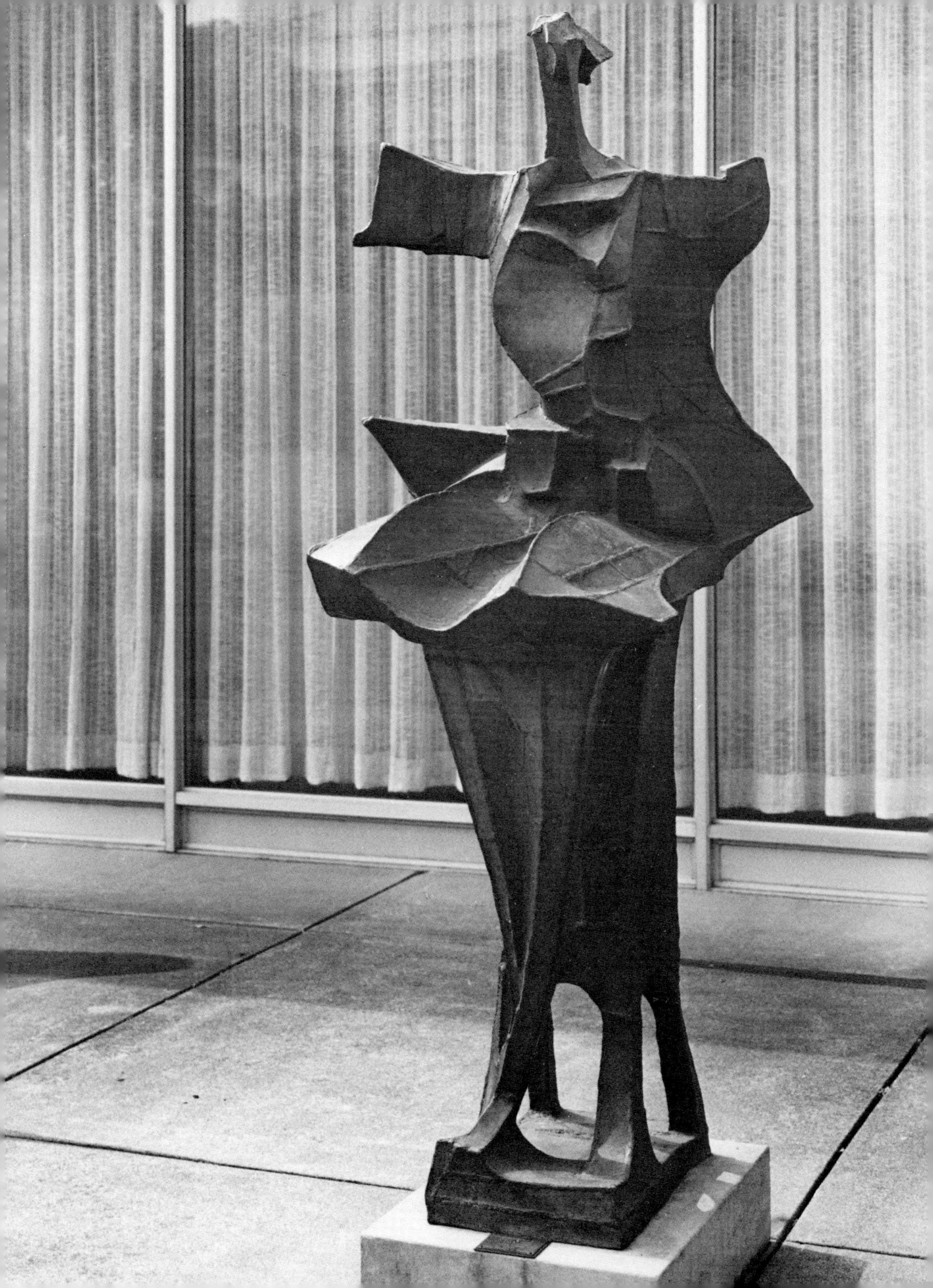

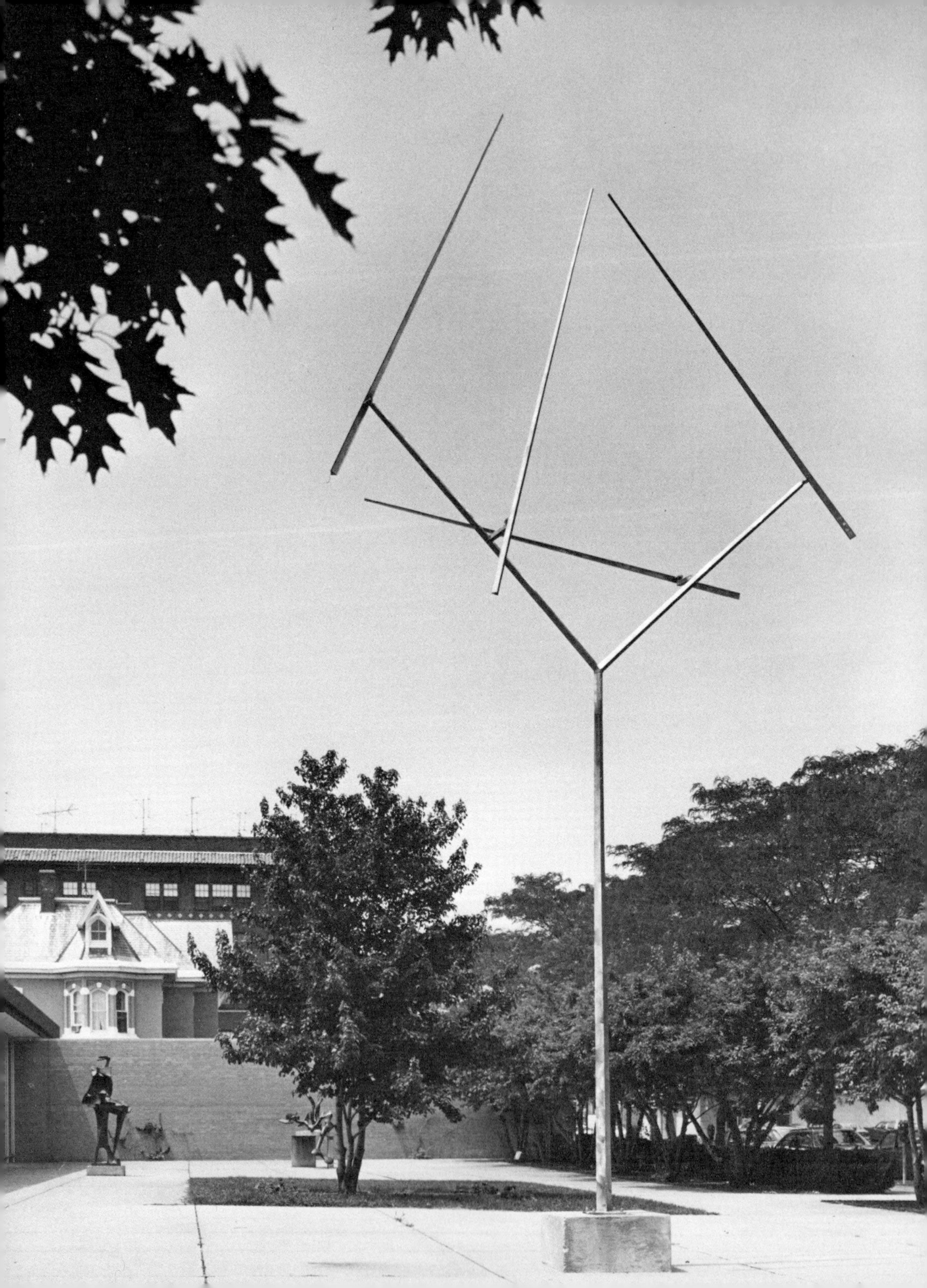

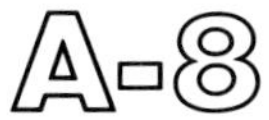

George Rickey (1907-   )

FOUR LINES OBLIQUE GYRATORY, VARIATION IV

1973, stainless steel, 26'-28'4"

Kalamazoo Institute of Arts
314 S. Park Street, Kalamazoo

Four Lines Oblique Gyratory, Variation IV, was commissioned for the site by Virginia Pratt Bardeen in memory of her mother, Evlyn Hall Pratt, who became acquainted with George Ricky when he was Director of the Kalamazoo Institute of Arts from 1939 to 1940. The kinetic sculpture is one of an edition of three; the second one was installed at the Max Plank Institute in Freiburg, Germany, in 1979. Set in motion by air currents, the ten foot oblique blades or lines gyrate around their axes forming ever-changing patterns in space. When the highly polished needlelike forms catch the light and the snow, they take on an eerie dissolution.

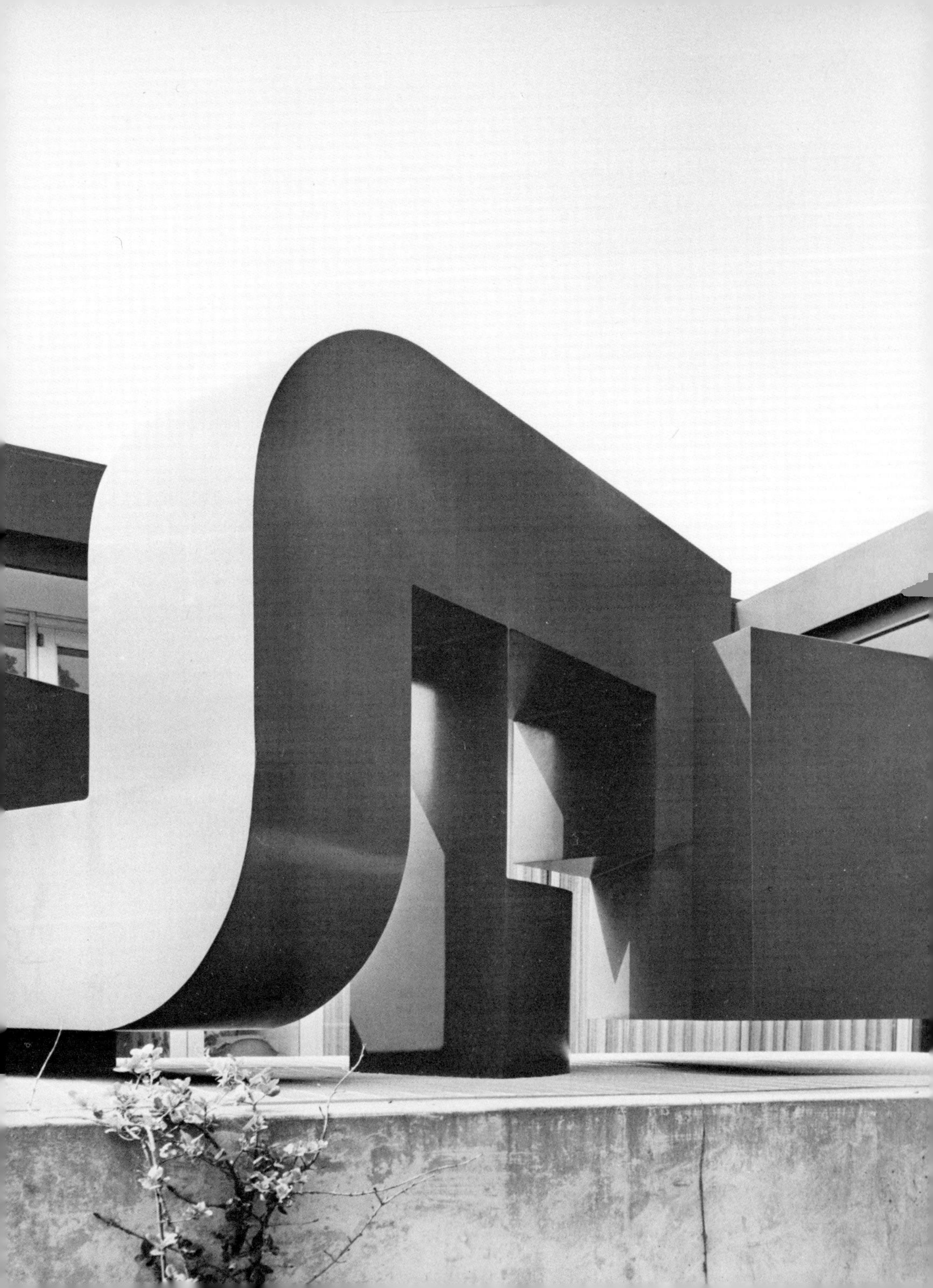

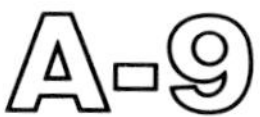

Jerald W. Jackard (Jacquard) (1937-   )

THE PASSING OF COLORED VOLUME

1968, aluminum, 6'5"

[Jaquard   68]

Kalamazoo Institute of Arts
314 S. Park Street, Kalamazoo

When the Kalamazoo Institute of Arts was constructed, the air shaft in the inner courtyard was designed to hold a sculpture. Jerald Jackard, formerly on the staff of the gallery, offered this work at the end of his one-man exhibition held at the Indianapolis Museum in 1976; the work was purchased at cost with funds from the 1975 and 1976 Art Auction. The sculpture is composed of large but simple volumes whose smooth surface planes are painted a luscious red. A sense of growth and energy passes through the connected volumes which reach out in several directions.

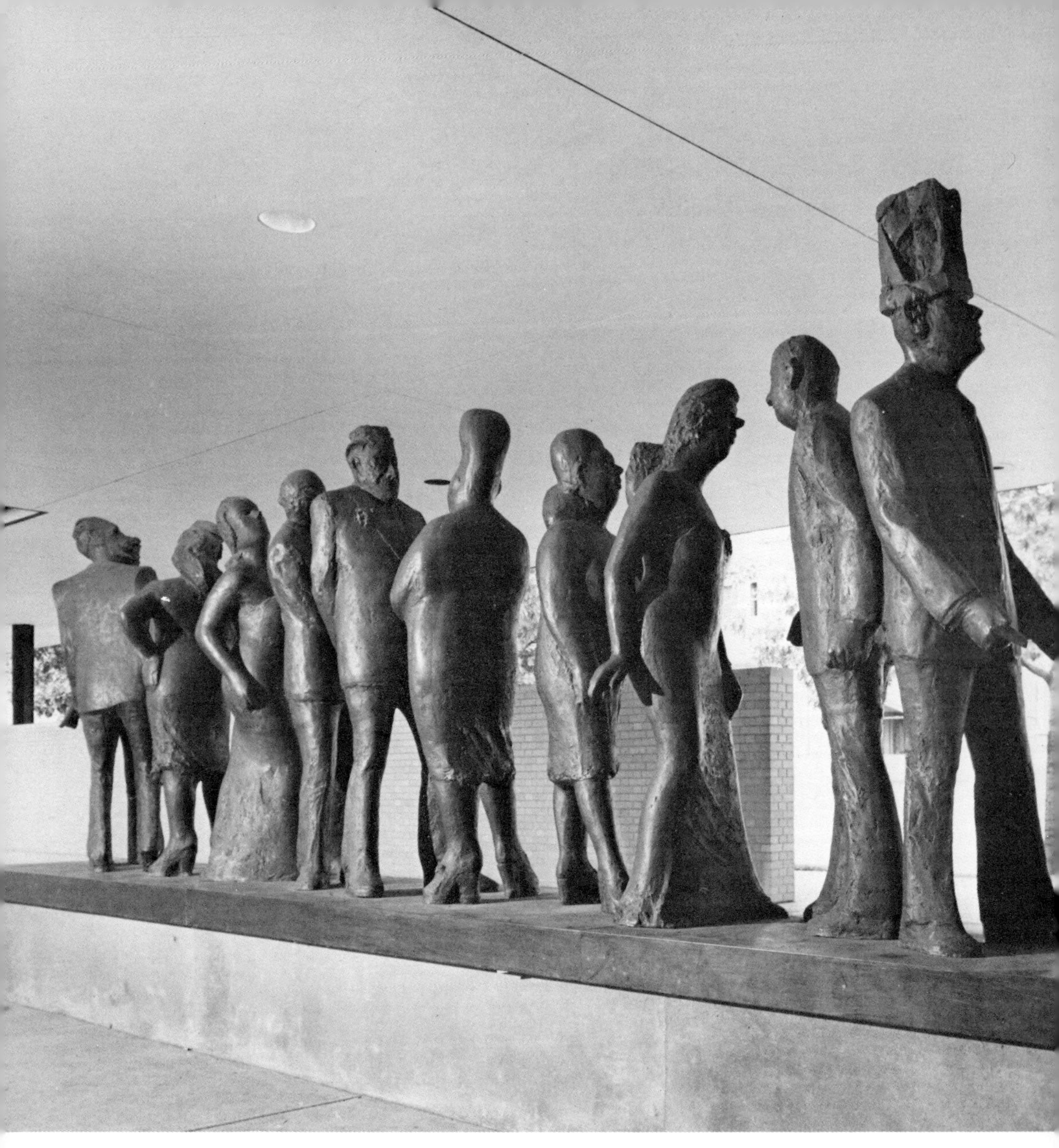

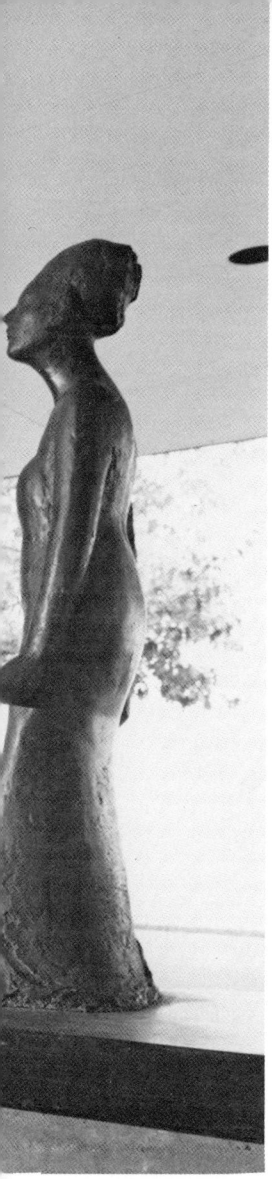

Kirk Newman (1926-   )
PEOPLE

1973-1974, bronze, c. 5'

Kalamazoo Institute of Arts
314 S. Park Street, Kalamazoo

People was commissioned by Mrs. Dorothy Upjohn Dalton to celebrate the fiftieth anniversary of the Kalamazoo Institute of Arts. The sculpture was unveiled on June 6, 1974, revealing an even dozen figures consisting of six men and six women. These thick, lumpy figures, who strike exaggerated poses, are a commentary on the social achievers in our society. Their dress, gestures, and other clues like a mask and a paper bag hat suggest that they have learned how to mask their real feelings while playing the game of success. While these figures point to corporate executives and society matrons, they also speak to basic human nature.

A-10

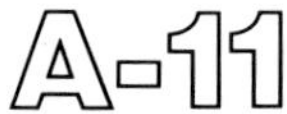

Alois Lang (1872-1954)   **(?)**

ANGEL

c. 1930, wood, c. 2'

First Presbyterian Church
321 W. South Street, Kalamazoo

When the First Presbyterian Church burned down, Philadelphia architect Charles Z. Klauder (1872-1938) was hired to design the present Gothic structure which was dedicated on April 13, 1930. The carvings found on the tympanum of the red entryway repeat the tracery and other motifs carved elsewhere on the building in stone. At the base of the tympanum is the bust of a golden, haloed angel carrying a shield. Since angels serve as God's messengers to man and as guardians, this angel may have been placed above the door to remind the worshipper of God's constant message of love and protection. The exterior decoration is tentatively attributed to the noted woodcarver Alois Lang, who is credited with the wooden carvings in the interior of the church.

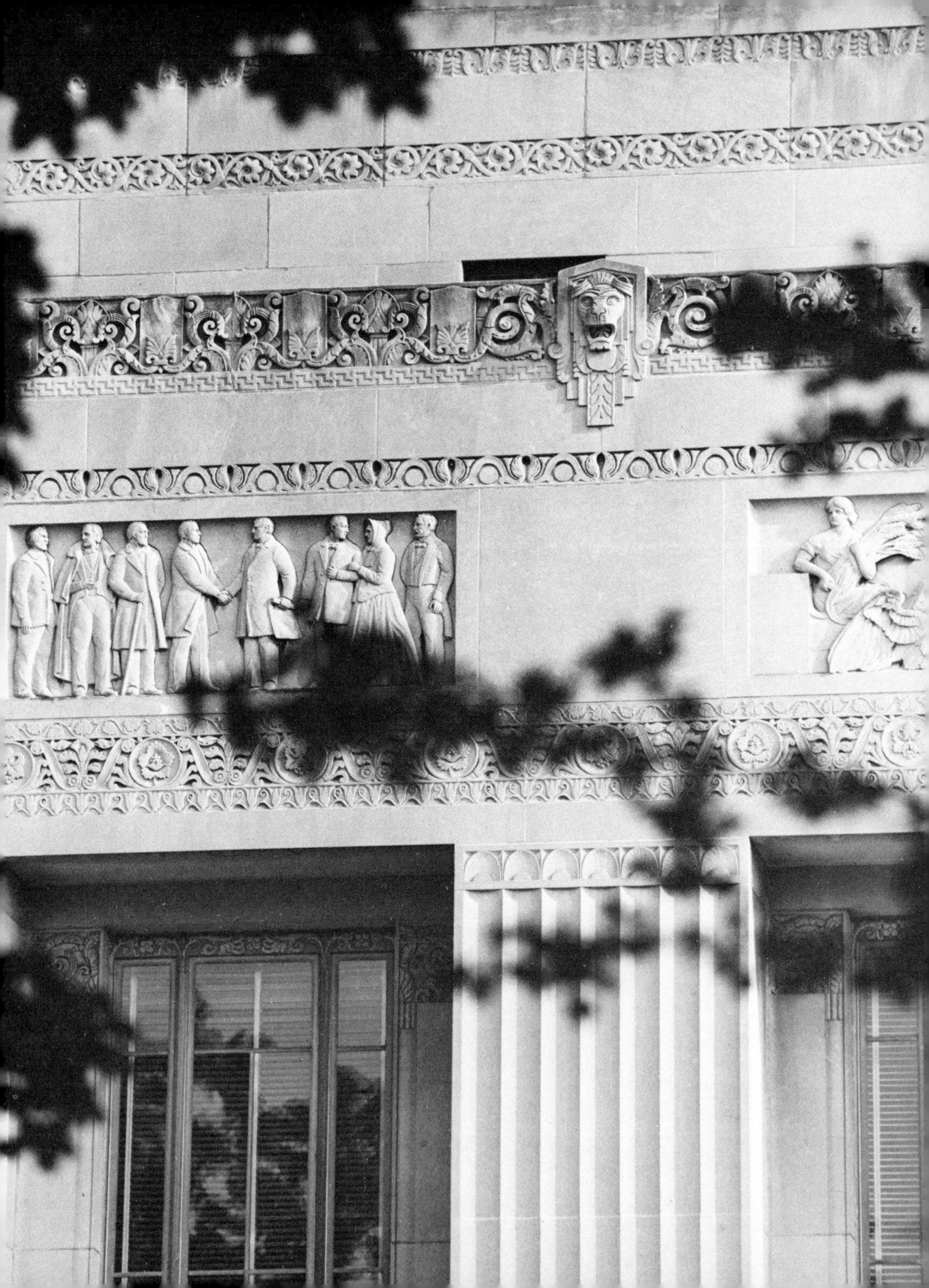

Studio of Architectural Sculpture
CITY HALL RELIEFS

1931, limestone, relief scenes c. 2'6"

City Hall
214 W. South Street, Kalamazoo

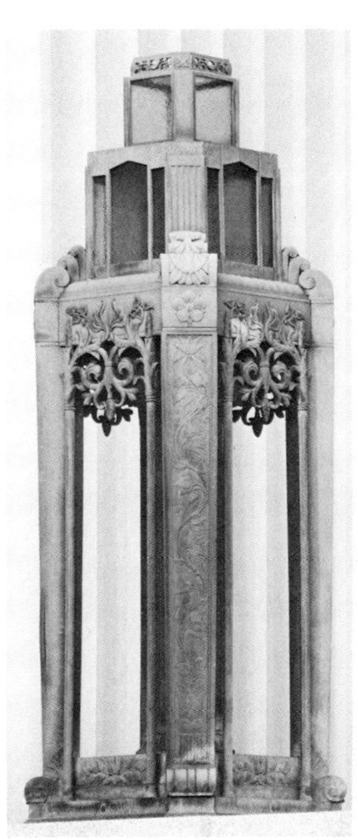

The dedication of the new streamlined City Hall, designed by the Chicago architectural firm of Weary and Alford, was held on September 1, 1931. The building is ornamented with relief panels and inscriptions which highlight the history of Kalamazoo. The inscriptions, selected by an inscription committee, include "Village Founded by Titus Bronson June 1829" and "First Newspaper 1835; Telegraph 1846; Telephone 1881." In addition to the list of inscriptions, the City Commission minutes for February 2, 1931, note that "it was also suggested that, so far as possible, the decorations of the exterior conform to the periods of these inscriptions, rather than to have clasic [sic] designs." The facade and rear of the building carry two pioneer scenes which flank two classical figures. The sides of the building carry two additional historical scenes. Floral and other motifs give horizontal and vertical emphasis to the building and decorate the lamps and flagpoles outside of the building.

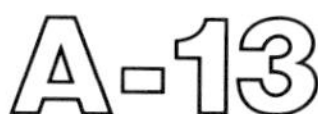

Artist Unknown

PARK CLUB DOOR RELIEFS

between late 1860s and 1880s, wood, 17"

Park Club (William S. Lawrence House)
219 W. South Street, Kalamazoo

The William S. Lawrence House, built in the late 1860s with a mansard roof, was remodeled into the picturesque Queen Anne Style in the 1880s. Lawrence was a partner in the firm of Lawrence & Chapin which manufactured agricultural implements and machinery. Lawrence's large home, which included a ballroom, was one of the social centers of Kalamazoo. The home passed through several owners before it was purchased by the Park Club, a private social club. The two carved faces surrounded by grapevines on the lower portion of the doorway repeat the carved grape motif found on the woodwork in the foyer. The door reliefs are reminiscent of the ancient god Dionysus, called Bacchus by the Romans, who was god of luxuriant fertility. He was especially associated with the grapevine, wine, and revelry. It is appropriate that the bacchanalian faces continue to grace the site of so many social activities.

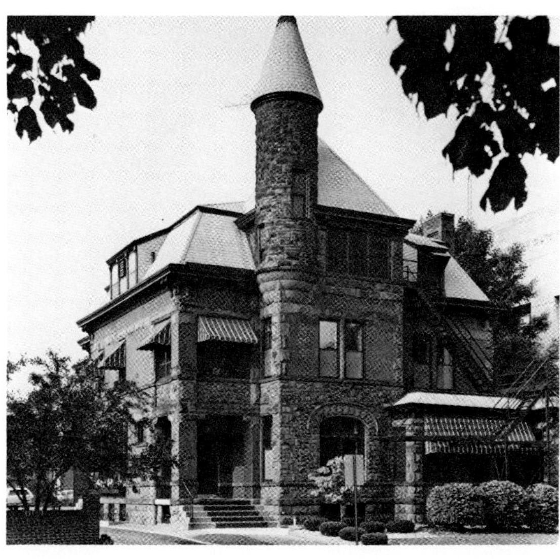

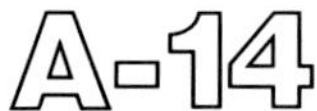

Artist Unknown (replica Leon E. Wallace)

GARGOYLE

c. 12th century, unknown metal, c. 18″ (replica 1978, copper)

Ladies Library Association Building
333 S. Park Street, Kalamazoo

The present gargoyle, which drains water from the porch of the Ladies Library Association Building, is a replica of the original gargoyle which may have been brought from England by Anna D. Clark, Dean of girls at Central High School. The building, designed by Chicago architect Henry L. Gay (1844-1921) and dedicated on May 20, 1879, was the first to be built in the United States by a women's club. Founded in 1852, the Ladies Library Association is also the oldest women's organization in Michigan. The Association grew out of a reading circle and later expanded its activities to include classes in history and other subjects, and guest lectures. Mrs. Lucinda H. Stone, one of the stalwart members of the association, also encouraged the formation of the Ladies Literary Club in Grand Rapids in 1869.

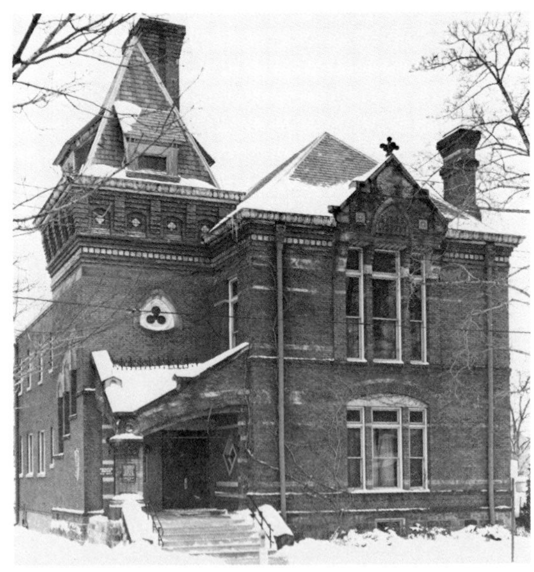

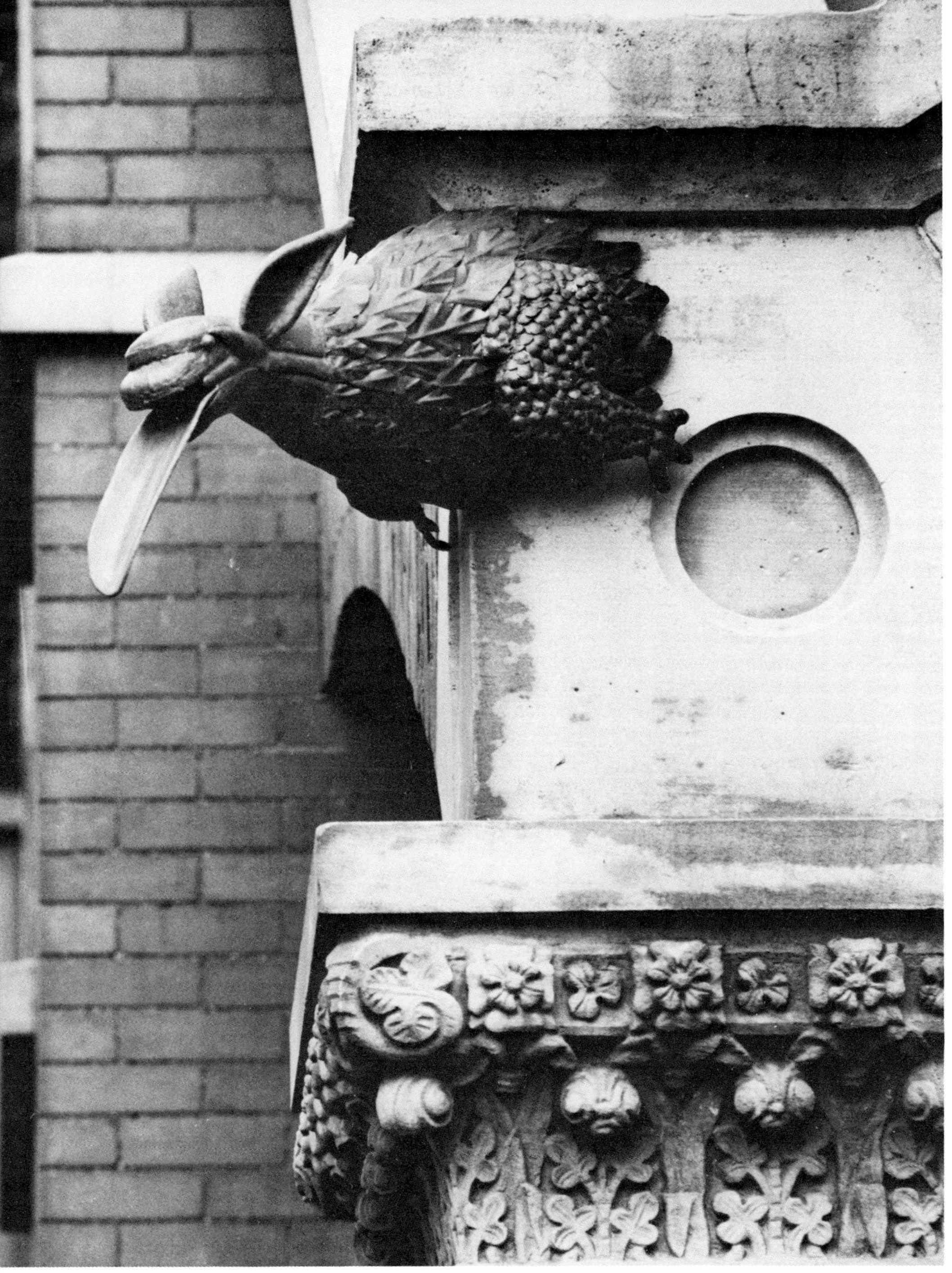

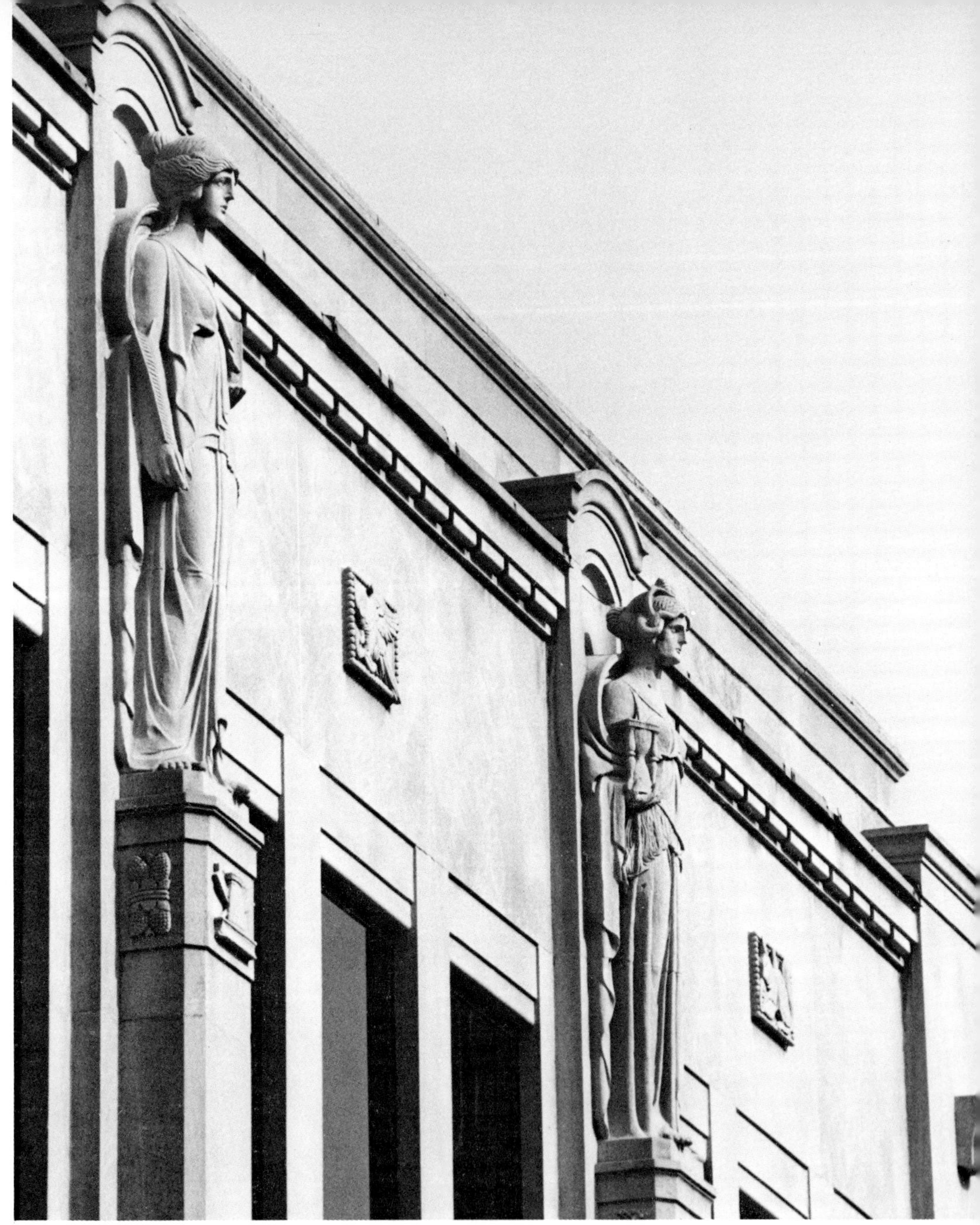

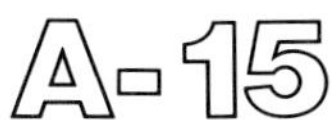

Artist Unknown

KALAMAZOO GAZETTE BUILDING RELIEFS

c. 1925, limestone, female figures c. 8'

Kalamazoo Gazette Building
401 S. Burdick Street, Kalamazoo

The sculptural reliefs on the Kalamazoo Gazette Building, designed by Detroit Architect Albert Kahn (1869-1942), refer to the history of printing and journalism. Near the top of the building facade are two classical females who stand atop pilasters. The figure on the left holds a quill pen and a book to record the events of time while the figure on the right holds an hourglass to mark the passing of time and a scroll. A printing press and other printing motifs can be found on the pilaster capitals. Below the cornice are masks at each corner and plaques which portray printer's marks and other symbols. Between the two figures is a plaque which "expresses what is perhaps the modern newspaper's principal duty. It shows a fabulous animal, half beast and half eagle, clutching in its mighty talons a writhing serpent, the traditional emblem of treachery against humankind. Vigilance conquering Iniquity— Vigilance over the public welfare!" (*Kalamazoo Gazette,* 18 October 1925: building sec., p. 1)

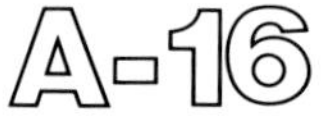

Artist Unknown

SETH THOMAS CLOCK

c. 1868, cast iron, c. 15′

Mackie and Ellis Jewelers
225 S. Kalamazoo Mall, Kalamazoo

The Seth Thomas cast iron clock has moved up and down Michigan Avenue and changed owners several times since it was placed in front of a jewelry store on what was known as East Main Street around 1868. The first owner may have been T. F. Pickering, who was an agent for Seth Thomas clocks and had a store at the corner of Main and Burdick. By 1890 the clock was owned by a clothier, Samuel Folz. The clock returned to the hands of a jeweler when it was purchased by Miron D. Ellis around 1924. It was moved about ten years later to 208 West Michigan and finally to the Mall in 1969 with the merger of Mackie and Ellis Jewelers. Originally equipped with a pendulum, the clock was converted to electricity around 1955 because its inaccuracy was creating havoc for downtown employees and shoppers. This early Seth Thomas clock, typical of nineteenth century civic improvements, has continued to charm and beautify Kalamazoo for more than one hundred years.

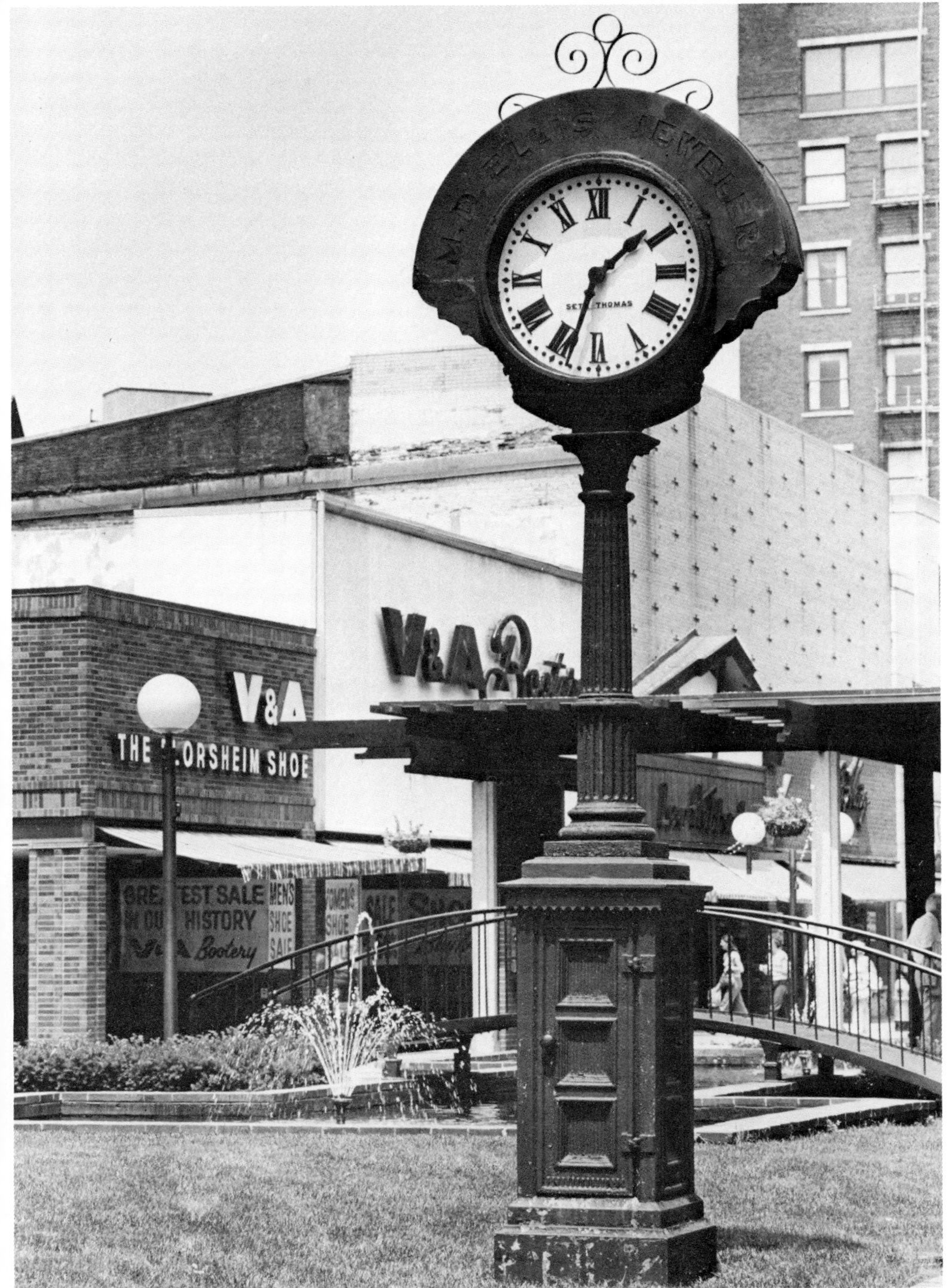
M. D. ELLIS JEWELER
SETH THOMAS
V&A
THE FLORSHEIM SHOE
V&A
GREATEST SALE
IN OUR HISTORY
Bootery
MEN'S SHOE SALE
WOMEN'S SHOE SALE
SALE

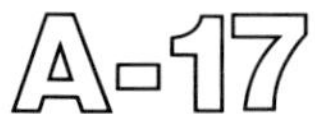

SCHAU-POWELL SPORT CENTRE RELIEFS

1886, terra cotta, limestone, sheet metal

Schau-Powell Sport Centre (Desenberg Building)
251 E. Michigan, Kalamazoo

In 1886, B. Desenberg & Co., wholesale grocers, moved from 108 Main Street into their new building at 227-231 Main Street, now 251 East Michigan Avenue. The firm, which was in business from 1860 until World War I, served hundreds of towns in Michigan and Indiana. It was reputed to be the heaviest tobacco jobber in the state and the first Michigan firm outside of Detroit to import tea directly from Japan. The Desenberg Building was designed by the Chicago firm of Adler & Sullivan and bears a close relationship to the Burnham and Root Rookery Building which was erected in Chicago shortly before. The ornamentation on the building reflects an important transitional stage between the early and mature styles of Louis Sullivan (1856-1924). Delicate spiral, s-shaped, and floral motifs decorate the limestone spandrels beneath the windows, the terra cotta friezes between the windows, and the sheet metal cornice and corner pinnacles.

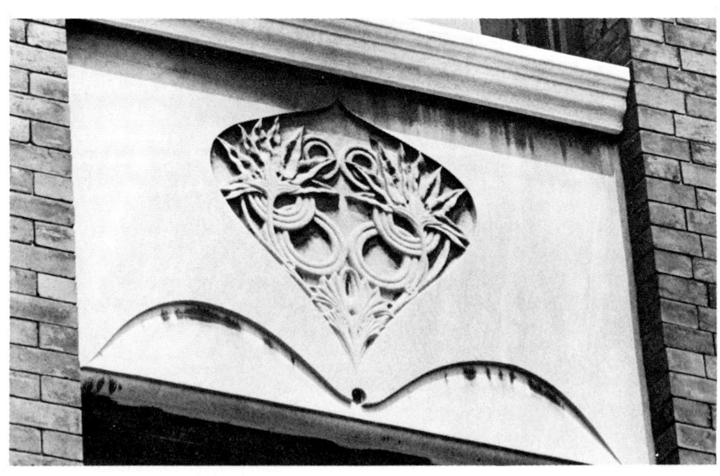

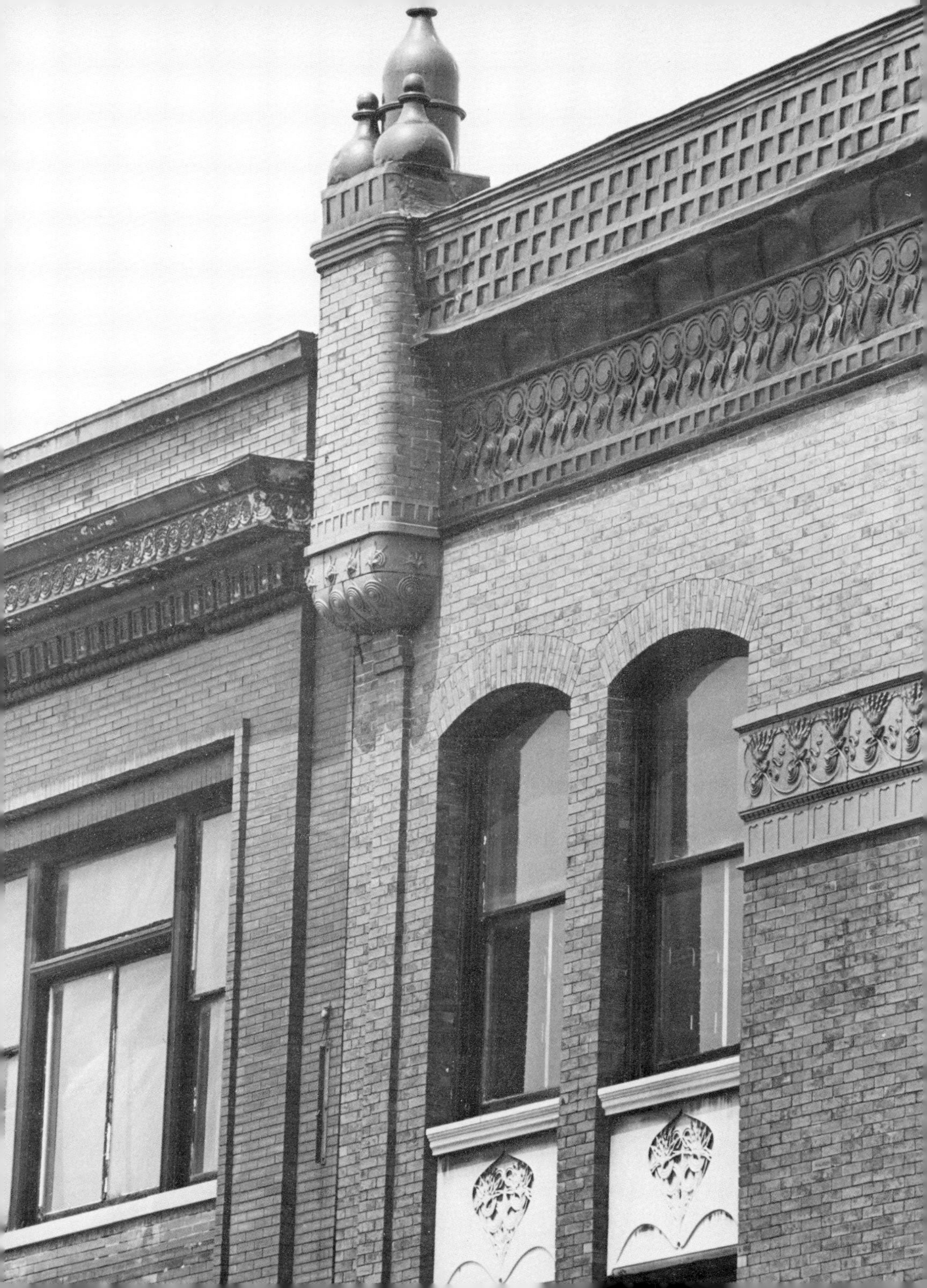

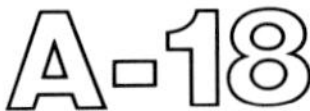

Douglas M. Gruizenga (1947-   )
INDUSTRIAL FORMS II

1974-1975, cor-ten steel, 10′

N. Kalamazoo Mall
between Eleanor and Water streets, Kalamazoo

Industrial Forms II was one of three sculptures which Douglas Gruizenga submitted to the 1974 River Bend Sculpture Competition in South Bend, Indiana. The winner of the competition was *Industrial Forms I; Industrial Forms II* was completed and given to the city of Kalamazoo by the artist. The piece is composed of smooth, abstracted forms which are basic to an internal combustion engine. The forms, shaped from the industrial material cor-ten steel, suggest the continual motion of an engine. Like others before him, Gruizenga celebrates the aesthetics of the machine, a basic component of our society.

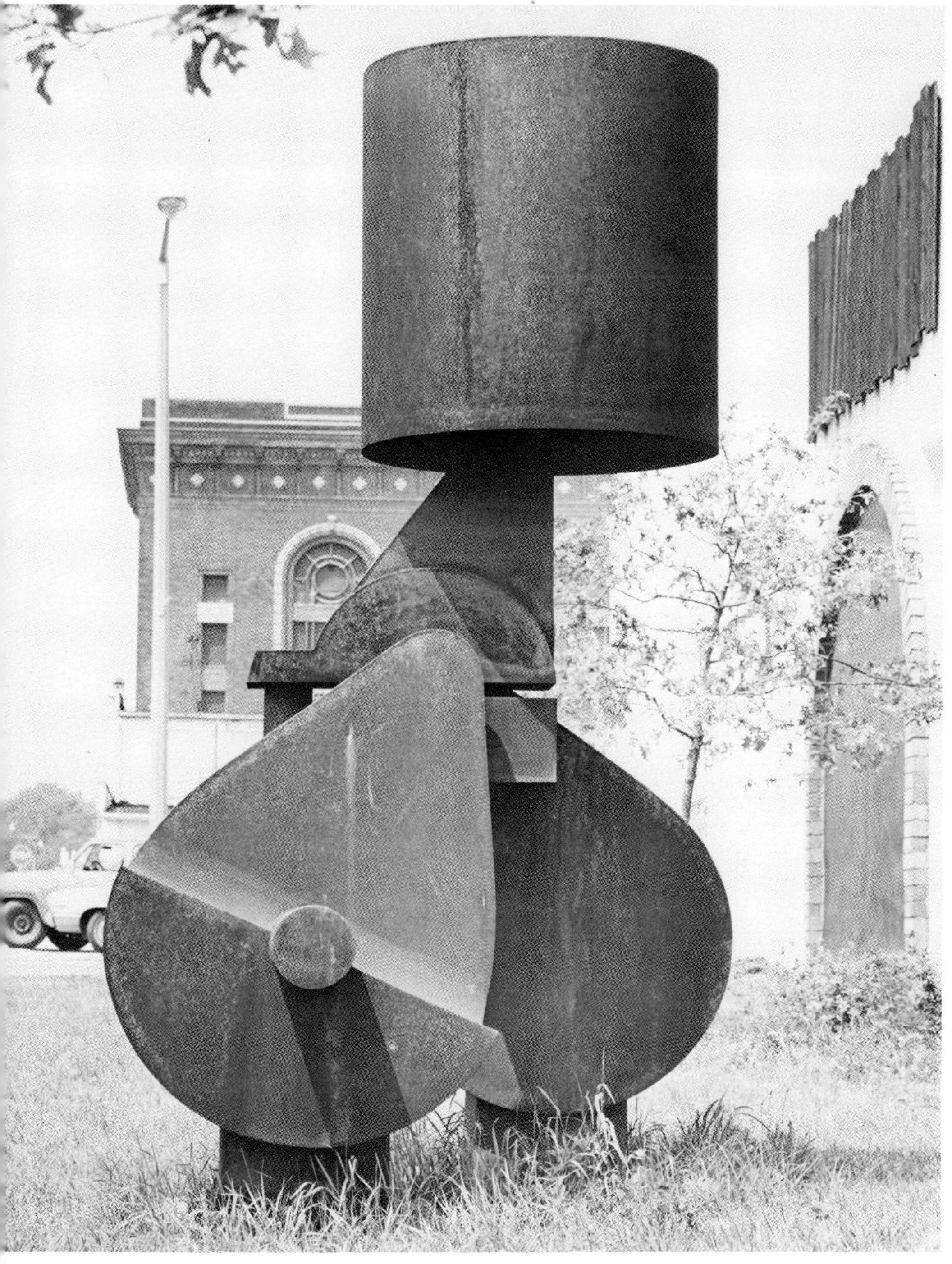

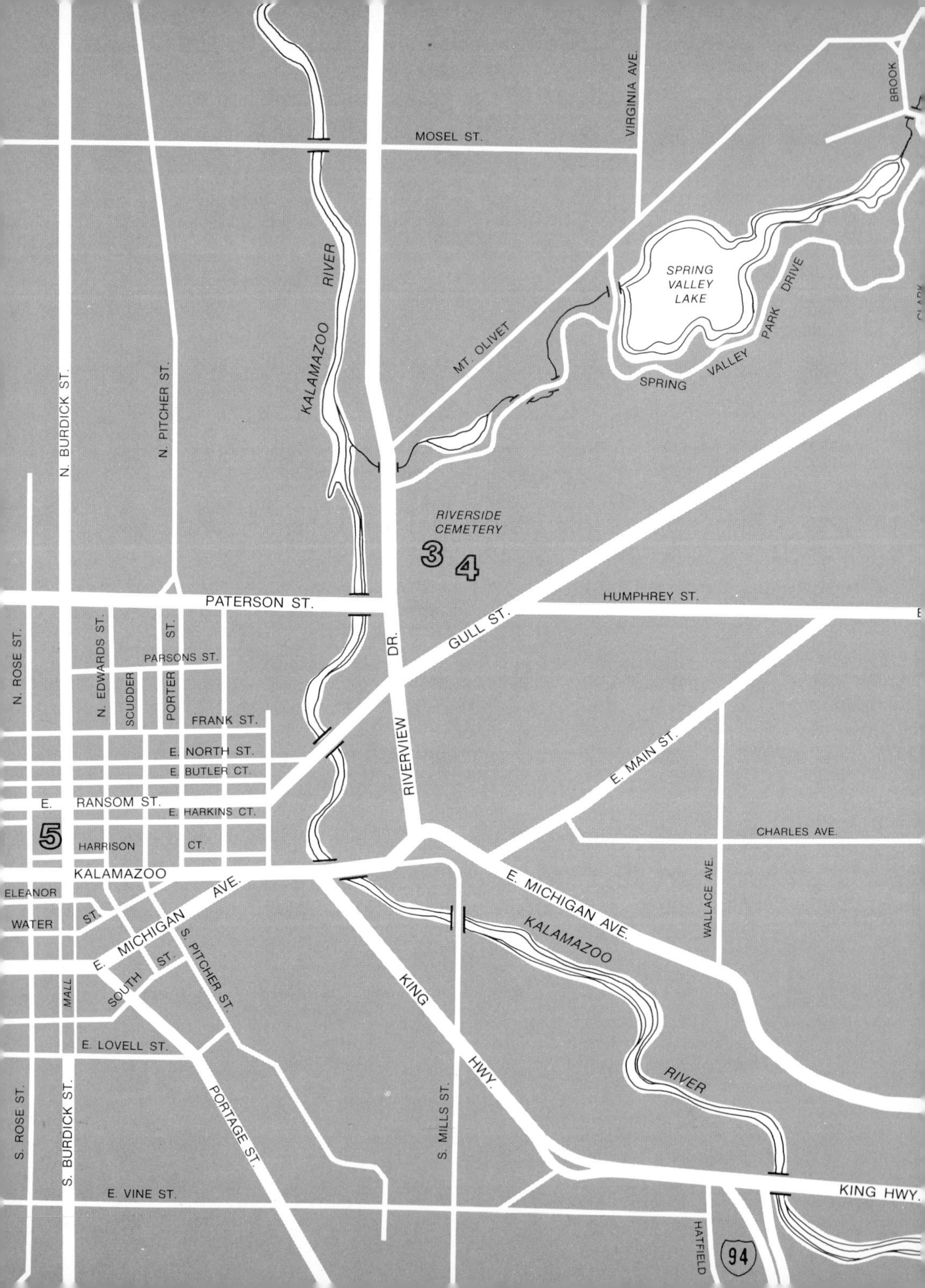

MOSEL ST.
VIRGINIA AVE.
BROOK
SPRING VALLEY LAKE
KALAMAZOO RIVER
MT. OLIVET
SPRING VALLEY PARK DRIVE
SPRING VALLEY
N. BURDICK ST.
N. PITCHER ST.
RIVERSIDE CEMETERY
3 4
PATERSON ST.
HUMPHREY ST.
GULL ST.
N. ROSE ST.
N. EDWARDS ST.
PARSONS ST.
PORTER ST.
SCUDDER
N. EDWARDS ST.
DR.
FRANK ST.
E. NORTH ST.
E. BUTLER CT.
RIVERVIEW
E. MAIN ST.
E. RANSOM ST.
E. HARKINS CT.
E.
5
HARRISON CT.
CHARLES AVE.
KALAMAZOO
WALLACE AVE.
ELEANOR
AVE.
WATER
E. MICHIGAN AVE.
ST.
E. MICHIGAN
KALAMAZOO
MALL
S. PITCHER ST.
SOUTH
ST.
KING HWY.
E. LOVELL ST.
RIVER
S. ROSE ST.
S. BURDICK ST.
PORTAGE ST.
S. MILLS ST.
E. VINE ST.
KING HWY.
HATFIELD
94

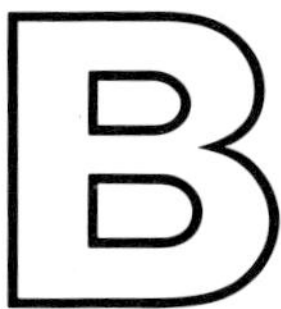

NORTHEAST

1. Bartholi (?), BISHOP BORGESS
   Nazareth College

2. Artist Unknown, GUARDIAN ANGEL
   Nazareth College

3. Artist Unknown, SOLDIERS' MONUMENT
   Riverside Cemetery

4. Pompeo L. Coppini, RICHARD B. WESTNEDGE
   Riverside Cemetery

5. James G. Jackson III, BLACK MADONNA
   Black Nationalist Church

6. Pompeo L. Coppini, GENERAL SHAFTER
   Charles Keck, U.S.S. MAINE MEMORIAL TABLET
   Galesburg

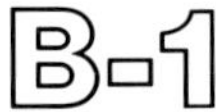

Bartholi (?)
BISHOP BORGESS

c. 1903-1905, granite, c. 60'

Nazareth College (Nazareth Academy)
1625 Gull Road, Kalamazoo

In 1870 Father Casper H. Borgess (1826-1890) became Bishop of the Diocese of Detroit, which at that time included all of the Lower Peninsula. Bishop Borgess was the benefactor and namesake of Kalamazoo's first hospital, Borgess Hospital. He died in Kalamazoo on May 3, 1890, while visiting a friend, Father Frank O'Brien. As Bishop Borgess had requested to be buried in Kalamazoo, his remains were temporarily buried in Father O'Brien's parish churchyard, Saint Augustine. Several years later the body was moved and a monument erected in Nazareth Woods, Nazareth Academy, which is operated under the auspices of the Sisters of Saint Joseph. The monument was dedicated amidst elaborate ceremonies on October 8, 1906. A newspaper article, "Dedication of Monument Monday" (*Kalamazoo Gazette*, 7 October 1906:5), states that the memorial is the work of Bartholi. In 1939, the body was reburied again in Sepulchre Cemetery, Detroit, with other deceased bishops of the diocese. The figure of Bishop Borgess, dressed in biretta (cap) and mozetta (cape), continues to give his blessing from high atop the Victorian monument.

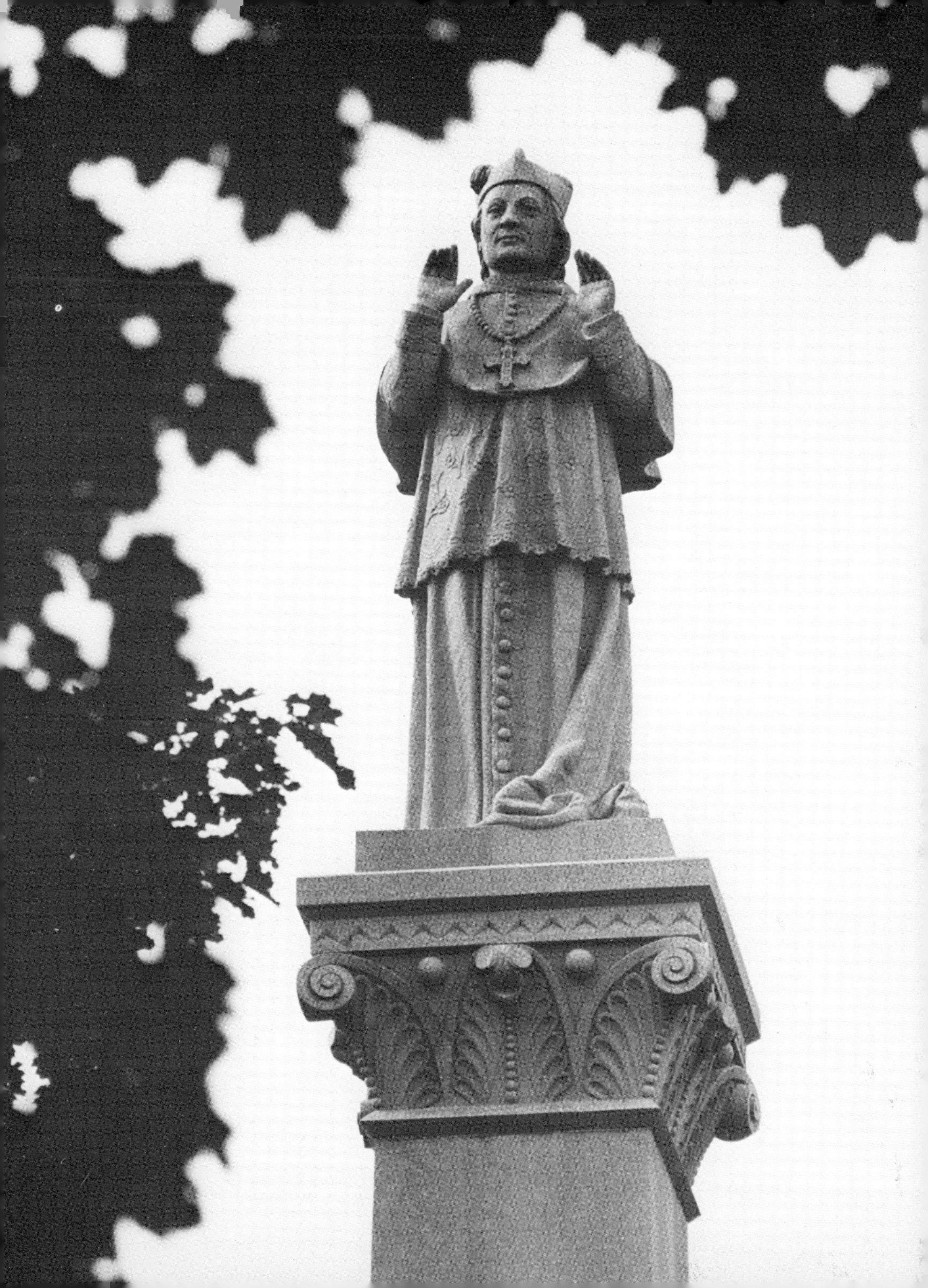

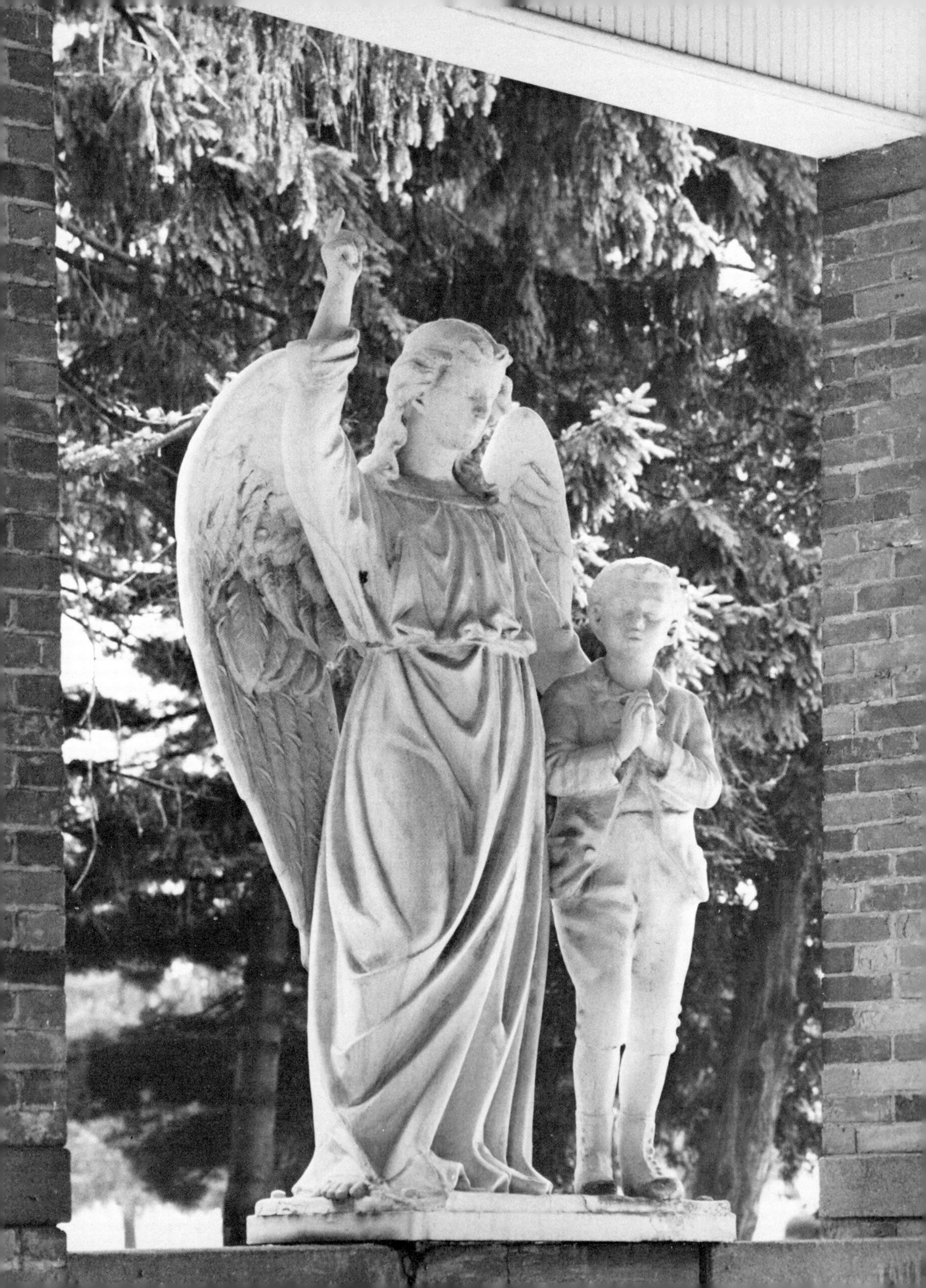

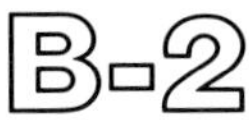

Artist Unknown

GUARDIAN ANGEL

c. 1891, nonferrous metal, 6′4″

Nazareth College (Nazareth Academy)
1625 Gull Road, Kalamazoo

On September 13, 1891, a monument and fountain were dedicated to Bishop Frederic Rese (1791-1871) by Saint Augustine Parish. Bishop Rese was the first Bishop of the Detroit Diocese which at that time included all of the Lower Peninsula. The monument was placed in front of LeFevre Institute, a parochial school administered by the Sisters of Saint Joseph. Now razed, both the school and Saint Augustine Church were originally located on Kalamazoo Avenue between Park and Cooley streets. Sometime after the turn of the century, the monument was moved to the grounds of Nazareth Academy (now Nazareth College), also administered by the Sisters of Saint Joseph. The sandstone base was placed near the monument to Bishop Borgess and the *Guardian Angel* was placed under the porte cochere of Barbour Hall, a boy's school. The young boy dressed in knickers and high top shoes, both with neat rows of buttons, and the angel serve as a reminder that God guides and protects each person through a guardian angel. In December of 1979, the *Guardian Angel* was removed from Barbour Hall before the building was razed and it will be relocated on the campus.

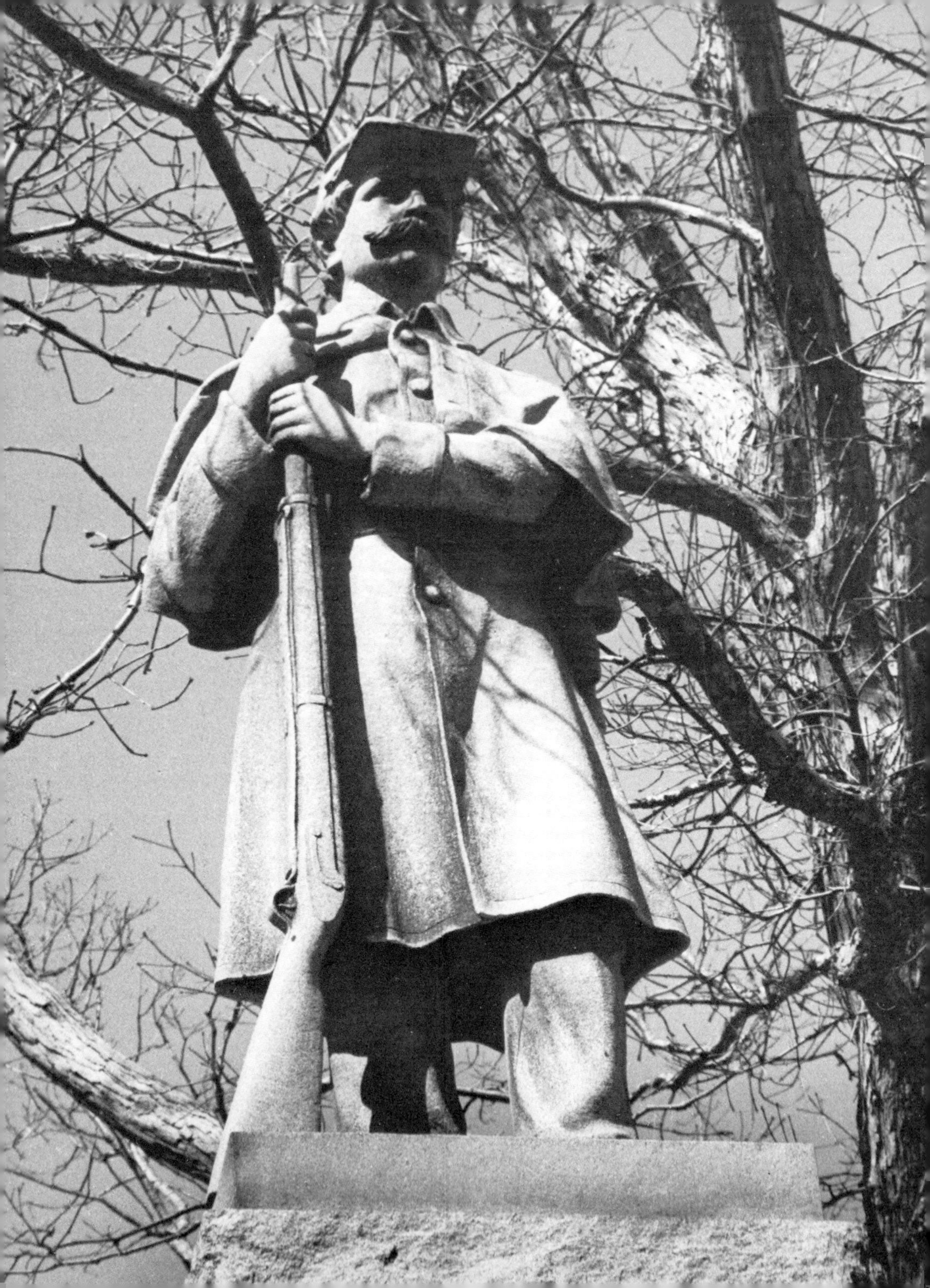

B-3

Artist Unknown

SOLDIERS' MONUMENT

c. 1901, granite, c. 30′

Riverside Cemetery
1015 Gull Road, Kalamazoo

The *Soldiers' Monument* was erected under the auspices of the Orcutt Post No. 79, G.A.R., to honor the private soldier who had fought in the Civil War. Dedicated on September 22, 1901, the monument is composed of a lone soldier atop a tall, roughly cut shaft. Though Civil War monuments generally appear quite similar to one another, the soldier is often an individualized figure. Here, a young, idealized soldier stands at ease, resting upon his rifle.

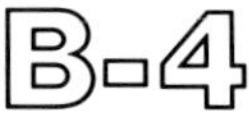

Pompeo L. Coppini (1870-1957)
RICHARD B. WESTNEDGE

1900, bronze, 28"

[Richard B. Westnedge   Surgeon 3rd Infty. U.S.A.
Coppini Sc.   1900   N.Y.   ? (illegible)]

Riverside Cemetery
1015 Gull Road, Kalamazoo

Richard B. Westnedge (1869-1899), surgeon in the Spanish American War, died in the Philippine Islands of typhoid fever. His mother, Mrs. Mary B. Westnedge, commissioned the memorial bust from the sculptor Pompeo Coppini, whom she had met in New York City at the First Christian Science Church. After receiving the bust, she displayed it in her parlor before placing it in Riverside Cemetery. Nestled beneath the floral motif which terminates Westnedge's uniform are the allegorical figures of *History* and *Patriotism.* Richard's brother, Colonel Joseph B. Westnedge, also fought in the Spanish American War. After the death of Colonel "Joe" during World War I, West Street was renamed Westnedge Avenue in honor of the two brothers who had given their lives in war.

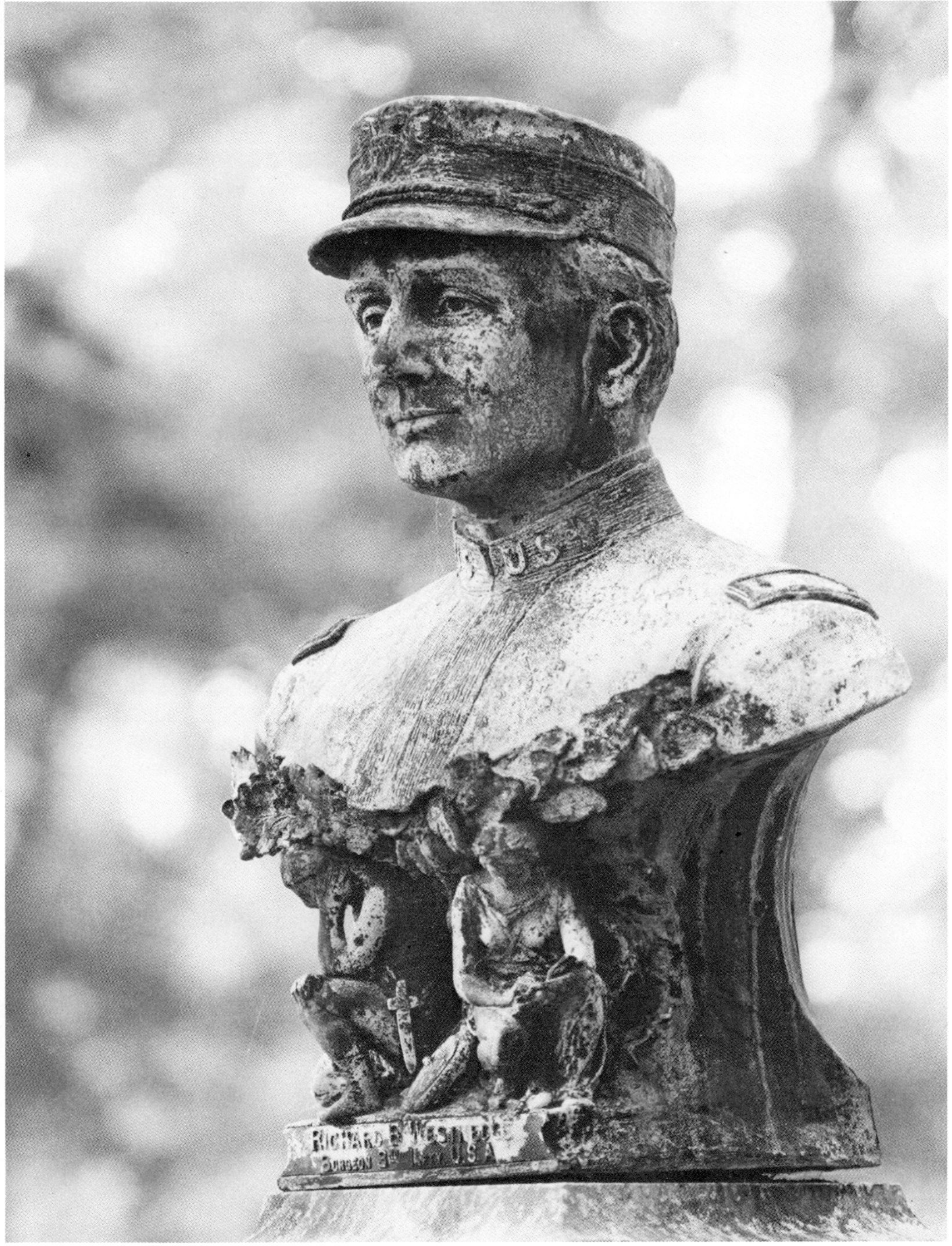

RICHARD B. WESTBROOK
SURGEON 3RD ... U.S.A.

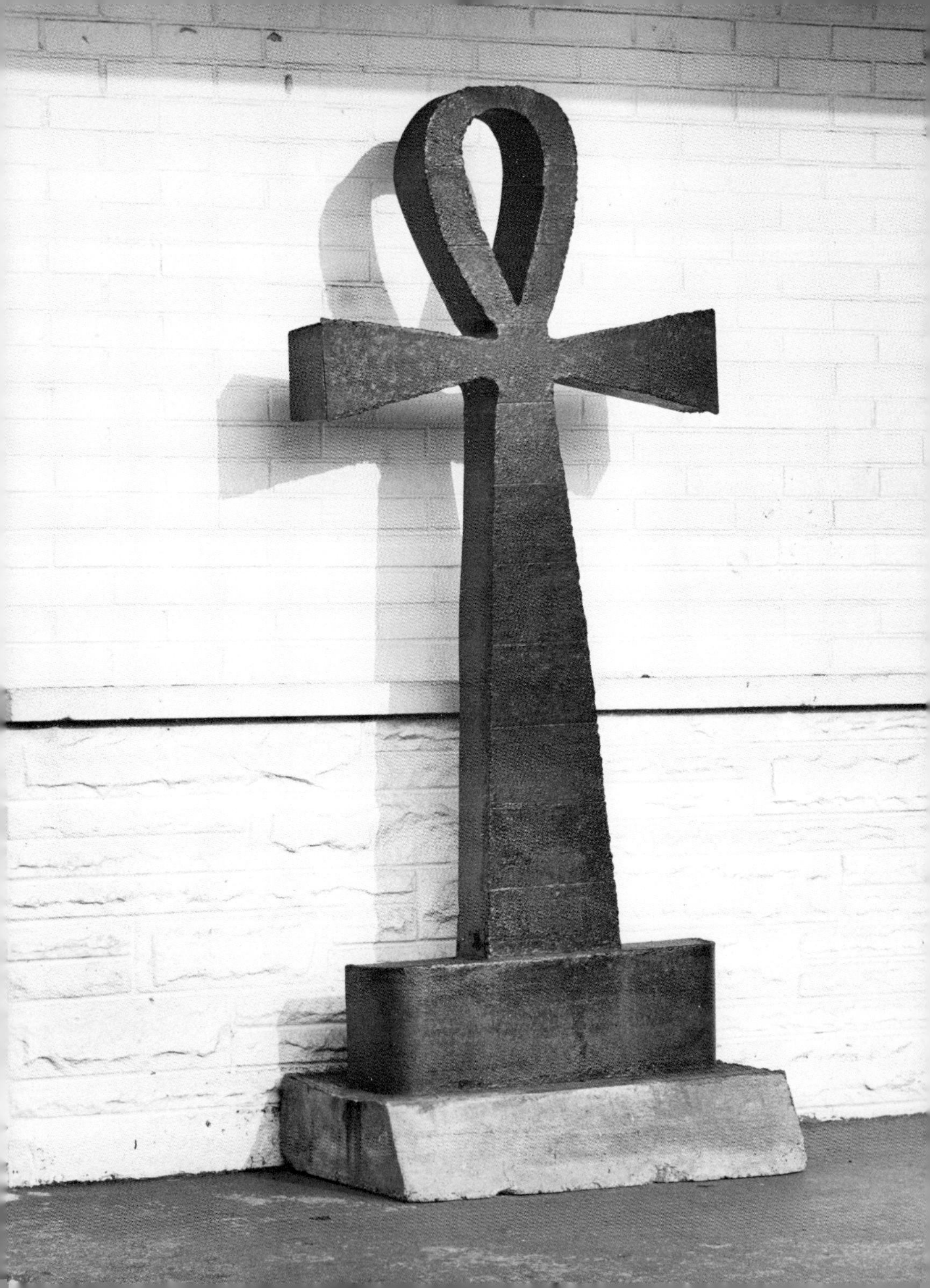

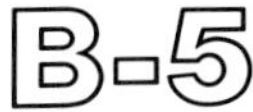

James G. Jackson III (1940-   )

BLACK MADONNA

1977, steel, 5′10″
[JGJ   III   77]

Shrine of the Black Madonna, Black Nationalist Church
1301 N. Burdick Street, Kalamazoo

The ankh, ancient Egyptian symbol of life, has been
chosen to symbolize the nurturer of Christianity,
Mary, the Mother of Christ. The ankh, composed of
welded steel which is tinted black, also refers to a
black Madonna and to the black woman as nurturer
of the family and black culture. The sculpture is
placed outside of the building which houses a church,
bookstore, and cultural center.

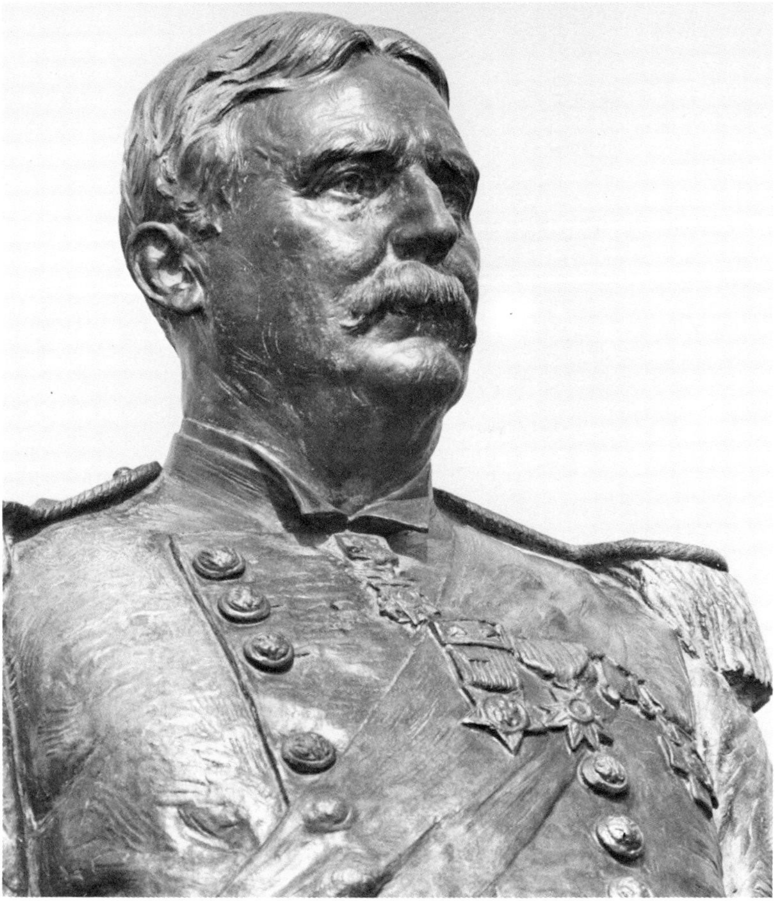

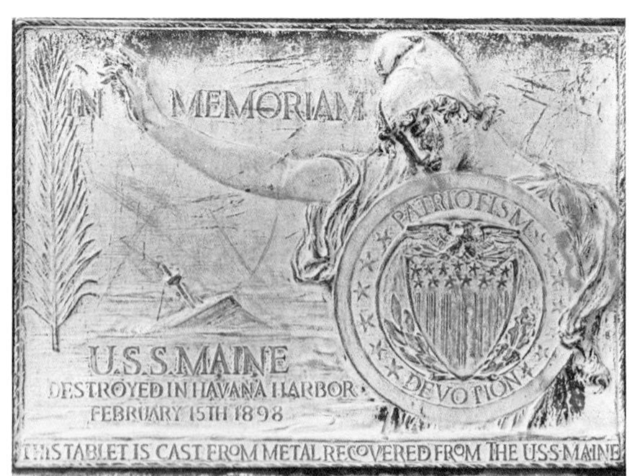

IN MEMORIAM
PATRIOTISM
DEVOTION
U.S.S. MAINE
DESTROYED IN HAVANA HARBOR
FEBRUARY 15TH 1898
THIS TABLET IS CAST FROM METAL RECOVERED FROM THE U.S.S. MAINE

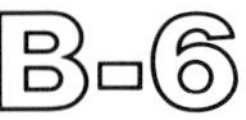

Pompeo L. Coppini (1870-1957)
GENERAL WILLIAM RUFUS SHAFTER

1919, bronze, 3'3"

[Pompeo Coppini Sc.   1919   Florentine Brotherhood Foundry   Chicago, Ill.]

Charles Keck (1874-1951)
U.S.S. MAINE MEMORIAL TABLET

1913, bronze, 13"

[©C. Keck Sc   1913   Cast by Jno. Williams Inc.   N.Y.]

M 96 and Michigan Avenue, Galesburg

The bust of General William Shafter (1835-1906) was commissioned by the State of Michigan through the General Shafter Monument Commission. Initially, an attempt was made to locate the bust in Lansing, but the legislature decided to erect it in Galesburg where Shafter had been born in a log cabin. Dedication ceremonies were held on August 22, 1919, followed by a ball game. The dignified bust portrays Shafter elegantly dressed in military uniform and bedecked with medals. Inscribed on the pedestal is Shafter's long military career, which includes the Civil War and the campaign against the Indians in the Southwest. At the base of the pedestal is Charles Keck's U.S.S. *Maine* relief which commemorates the Spanish American War in which Shafter played an important role. Another casting of the relief is located in Bronson Park (see p. 20). On August 19, 1941, a collision caused the bust to be hurled from its pedestal. The monument was returned to the center of Galesburg in the spring of 1942.

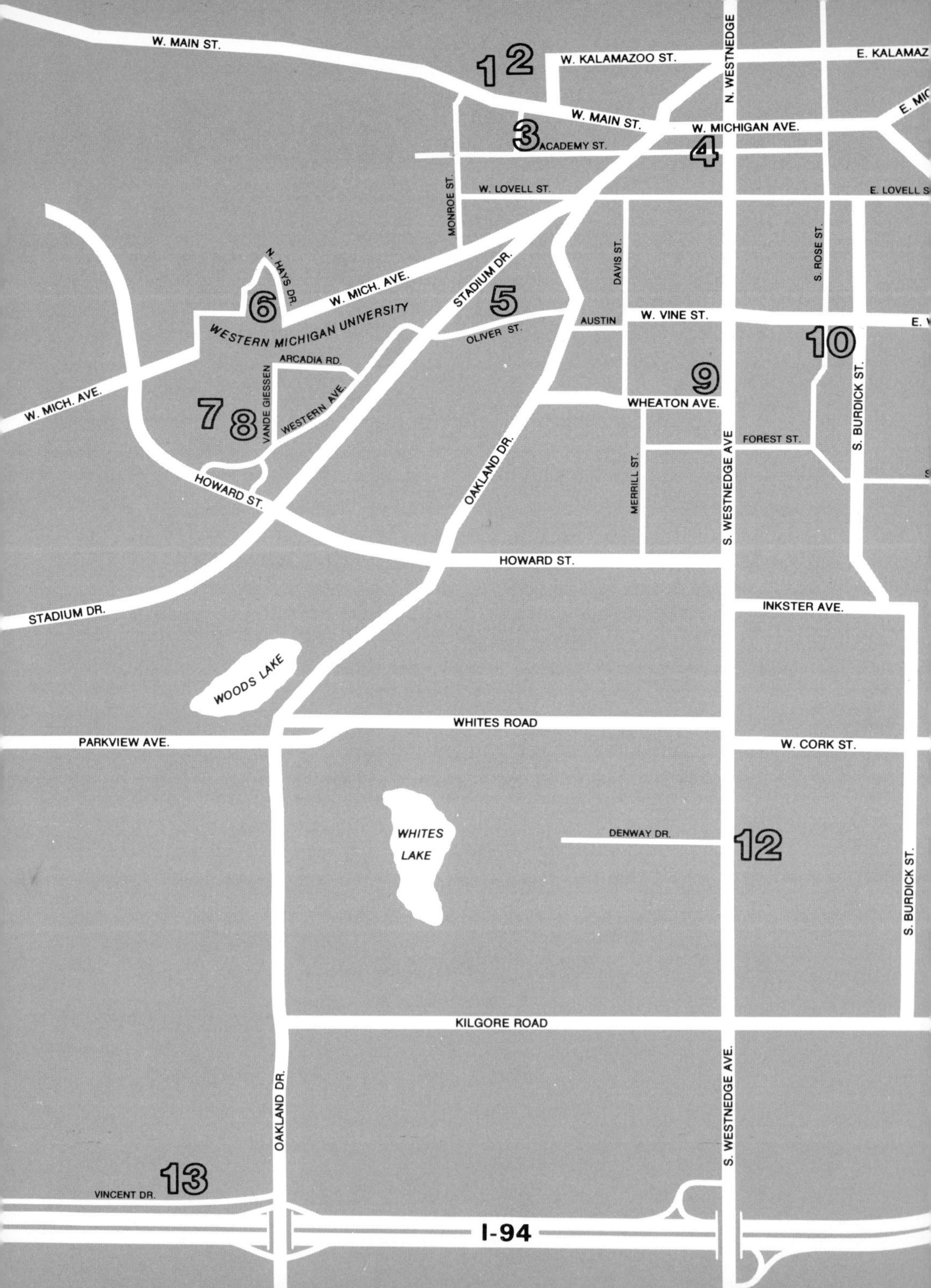

W. MAIN ST.
W. KALAMAZOO ST.
E. KALAMAZ
N. WESTNEDGE
W. MAIN ST.
W. MICHIGAN AVE.
E. MI
ACADEMY ST.
W. LOVELL ST.
E. LOVELL S
MONROE ST.
DAVIS ST.
S. ROSE ST.
N. HAYS DR.
W. MICH. AVE.
STADIUM DR.
WESTERN MICHIGAN UNIVERSITY
OLIVER ST.
AUSTIN
W. VINE ST.
E.
ARCADIA RD.
VANDE GIESSEN
WESTERN AVE.
WHEATON AVE.
S. BURDICK ST.
FOREST ST.
W. MICH. AVE.
OAKLAND DR.
MERRILL ST.
S. WESTNEDGE AVE.
HOWARD ST.
HOWARD ST.
INKSTER AVE.
STADIUM DR.
WOODS LAKE
WHITES ROAD
PARKVIEW AVE.
W. CORK ST.
WHITES LAKE
DENWAY DR.
S. BURDICK ST.
KILGORE ROAD
OAKLAND DR.
S. WESTNEDGE AVE.
VINCENT DR.
I-94

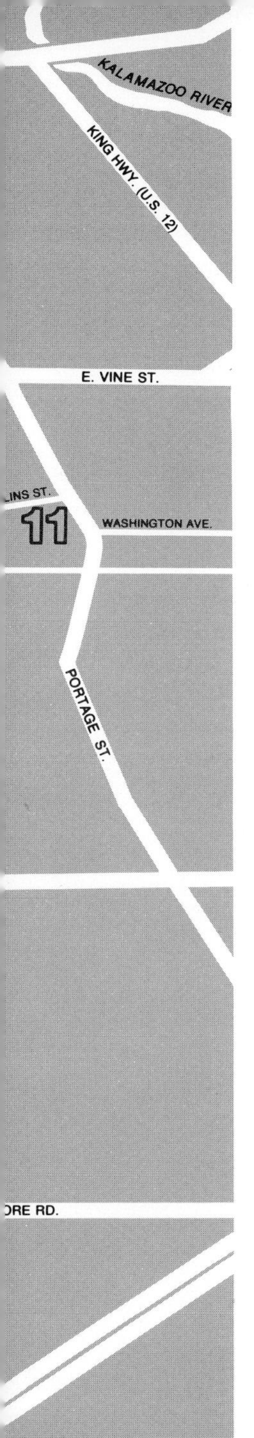

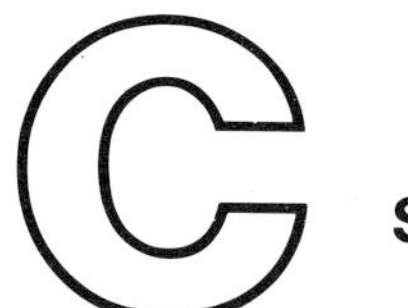

SOUTHWEST

1. Artist Unknown, ANGELS
   Mountain Home Cemetery

2. Artist Unknown, HOPE, MCCORTIE MONUMENT
   Mountain Home Cemetery

3. Bernard S. Palchick, DÉTENTE
   Kalamazoo College

4. Artist Unknown, SAINT AUGUSTINE
   Saint Augustine Church

5. Artist Unknown, LAVINIA SPINDLER HALL RELIEFS
   Western Michigan University

6. Douglas M. Gruizenga, UNTITLED
   Western Michigan University

7. Carole Harrison, THREE FIGURES
   Western Michigan University

8. Gerald C. Dumlao, SUN DISC
   Western Michigan University

9. Carole Harrison, FOUNTAIN
   Steinman-Dudley Company

10. After Luca della Robbia, TRUMPETERS, DRUMMERS from the CANTORIA
    Zelinger House

11. Artist Unknown, "BOY READING A BOOK"
    Washington Square Library

12. Bernhard Zuckermann, THE WADERS
    Mount Ever-Rest Memorial Park

13. Leo Lentelli, COMMERCE, AGRICULTURE; INDUSTRY, ARTS
    Cathedral Church of Christ the King

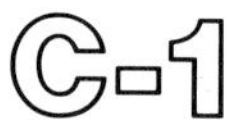

Artist Unknown

ANGELS

1878, sandstone, 10″

Chapel, Mountain Home Cemetery
1402 W. Main Street, Kalamazoo

The Mountain Home Cemetery Association was incorporated on March 28, 1849, to provide for burial outside of the city in a picturesque rural cemetery. In 1878 a charming Gothic chapel was erected near the entrance to the grounds. Large leaves inch their way up the gable which is surmounted by a cross. Weathered angels terminate the moulding around the doorway. The angel on the right holds a shield decorated with a cross while the one on the left holds an open book. These emissaries of God are a reminder that those who follow God's word will receive His protection and find their names recorded in the Book of Life. They follow the ancient tradition established by King Solomon who had cherubim carved on the doors of the Temple.

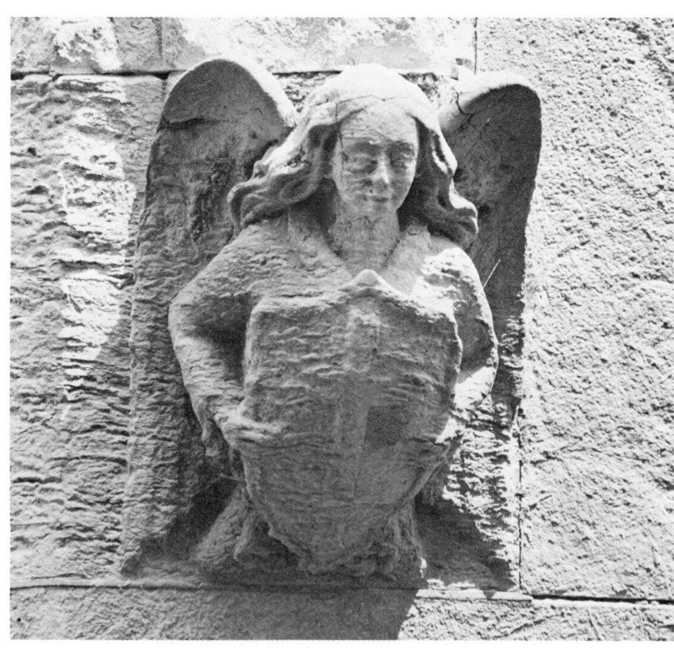

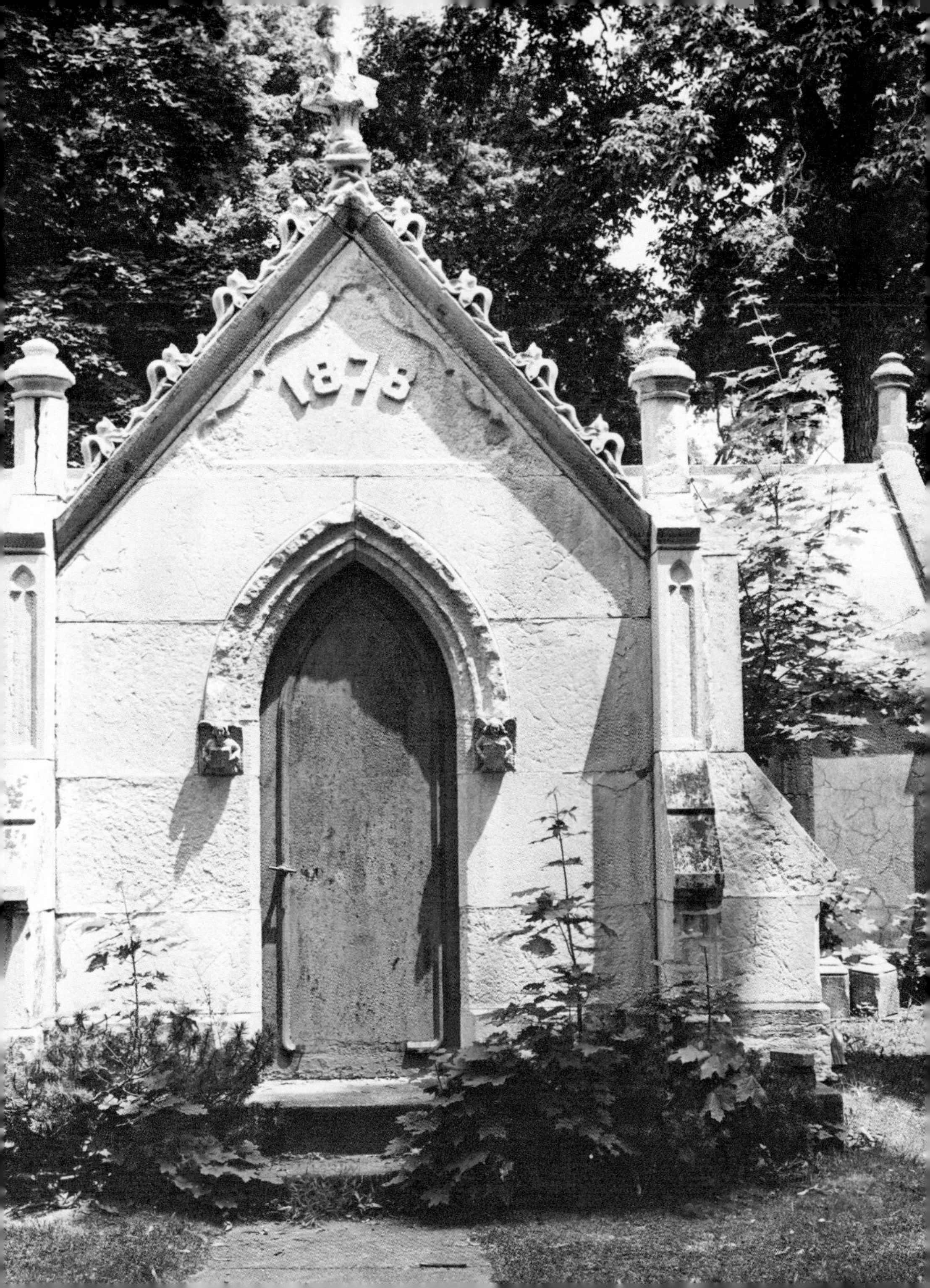

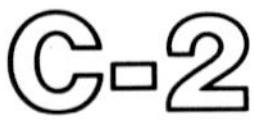

Artist Unknown

HOPE, MCCORTIE MONUMENT

before 1887, marble, 5'2"

Mountain Home Cemetery
1402 W. Main Street, Kalamazoo

The McCortie Monument was quite likely erected after the death of Amanda M. Wayne McCortie (1832-1868) by her husband, William H. (1833-1923). It was in place by 1887, since a drawing of it appeared in the *Kalamazoo Daily Telegraph Trade Edition* (p. 4). A classically draped figure of *Hope* looks heavenward while her left hand rests on an anchor now partially destroyed. The anchor as a symbol of hope and steadfastness is referred to in Hebrews 6:19: "Which hope we have as an anchor of the soul, both sure and steadfast..." The figure of *Hope* is a reminder to Christians that the steadfast soul will be rewarded after death with everlasting life.

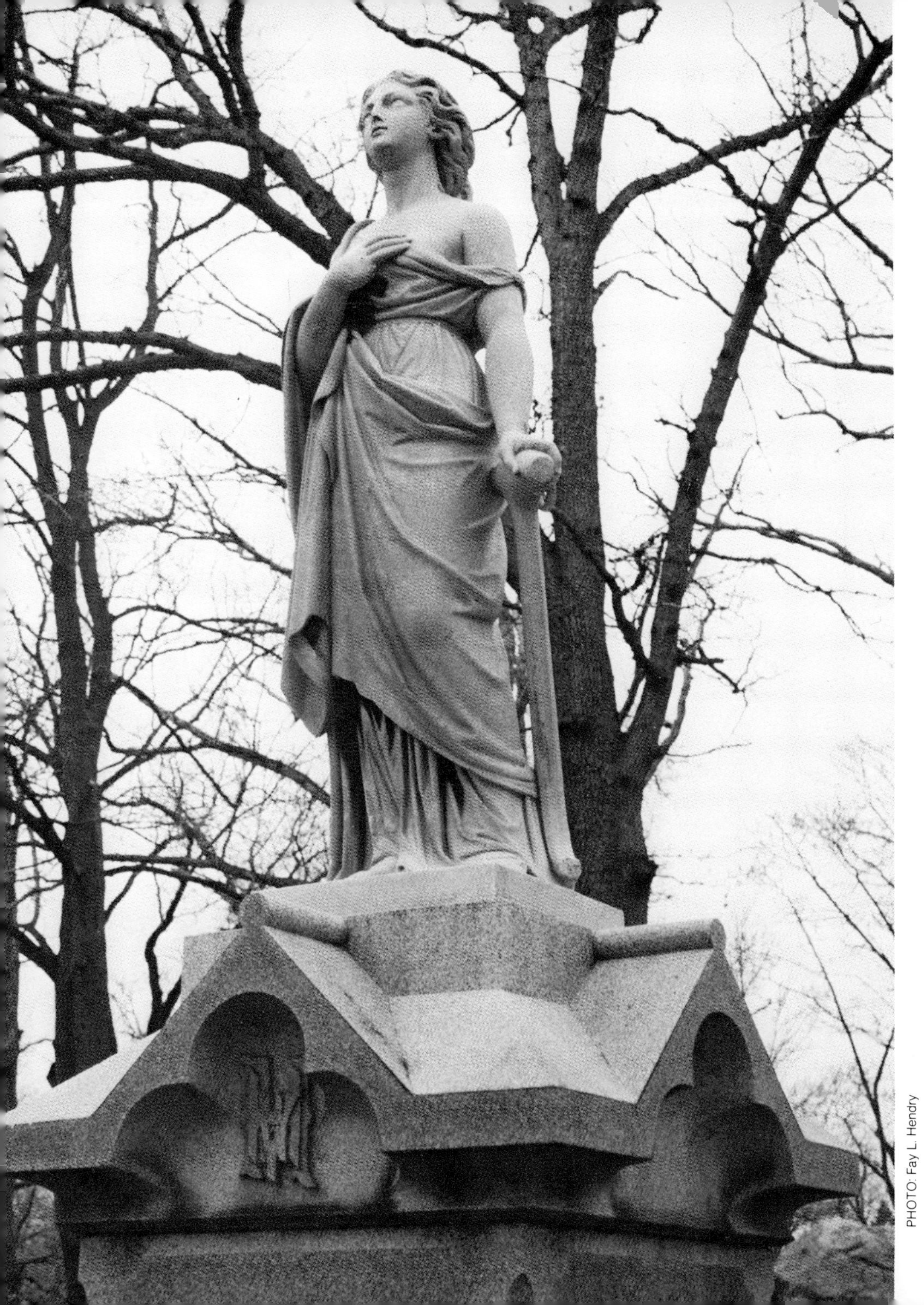

PHOTO: Fay L. Hendry

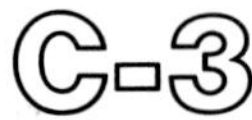

Bernard S. Palchick (1945-   )
DÉTENTE

1973, steel, 4'4"
[BSP   73]

Light Fine Arts Building, Kalamazoo College
1200 Academy Street, Kalamazoo

Détente was created by Bernard Palchick through a
Faculty Development Grant awarded by
Kalamazoo College in 1973. The vertical portion
of the sculpture forms a triangle from which
three long legs run horizontally along the ground
seemingly in pursuit of each other. The relaxed
tension of this work, which is painted blue,
reflects the title of the sculpture and the political
popularity of the word détente in the 1970s.

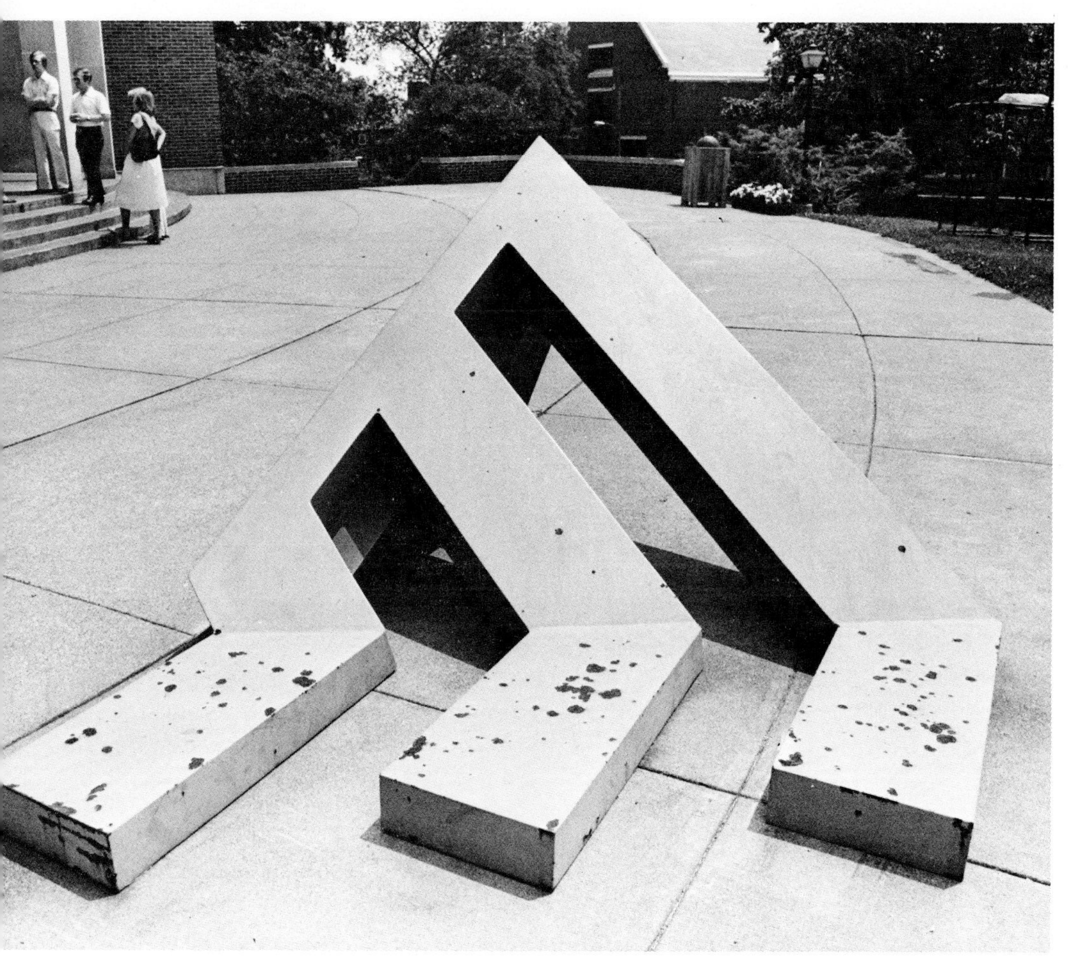

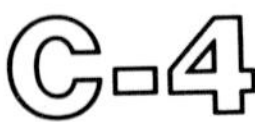

Artist Unknown
SAINT AUGUSTINE

date unknown, nonferrous metal, 6'
[N. SERF   MANUF NY]

Saint Augustine Church
542 W. Michigan Avenue, Kalamazoo

The statue of Saint Augustine appears to have originally been placed in a niche on the facade of LeFevre Institute after it was erected in 1891. This elementary school and the old Saint Augustine Church were located on Kalamazoo Avenue between Park and Cooley streets before being razed in the 1950s. Saint Augustine, one of the early Church Fathers and Bishop of Hippo in Africa, is patron saint of Saint Augustine Parish which was founded over one hundred years ago. In 1957 the Najera Caravan, Order of Alhambra, placed a commemorative plaque on the pedestal in remembrance of the first recorded mass said in the area. According to the plaque, mass was held by the missionary Father Louis J. DeSeille in the home of Dennis Talbot on August 28, 1832. Dressed in a mitre (hat) and an elegantly embroidered cape, Saint Augustine raises his right hand in a perpetual blessing. His left hand may originally have held a staff.

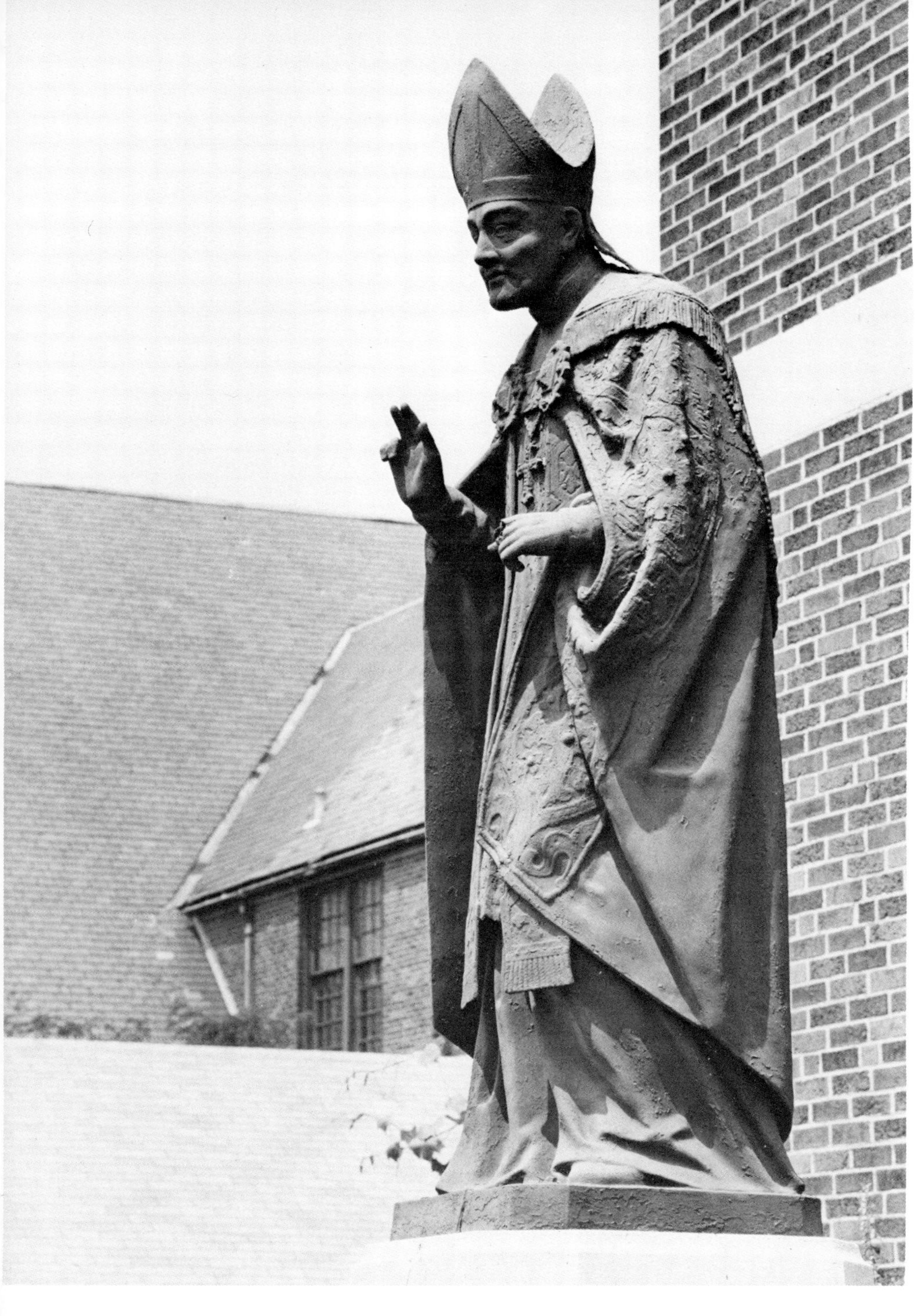

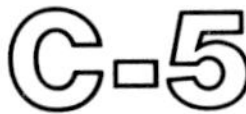

Artist Unknown

LAVINIA SPINDLER HALL RELIEFS

1940, limestone, 2′

Lavinia Spindler Hall for Women, Western Michigan University
Oliver Street, Kalamazoo

Dedication ceremonies for the Lavinia Spindler Hall, a dormitory for women, were held October 17-19, 1940. The building, designed by the Detroit firm of Malcomson, Calder and Hammond, was named after Lavinia Spindler who had been a faculty member at what was formerly known as Western Michigan Teachers College. The flanking reliefs above the doorway were created through the Work Projects Administration, Federal Works Agency. They describe the contributions that Miss Spindler made to the school between 1907 and 1939, including her role as critic-teacher, director of the training school, dean of women, and freshman advisor. The simplified blocklike figures with incised linear details are typical of the Art Deco style which became progressively less angular and geometric in the 1940s and 1950s.

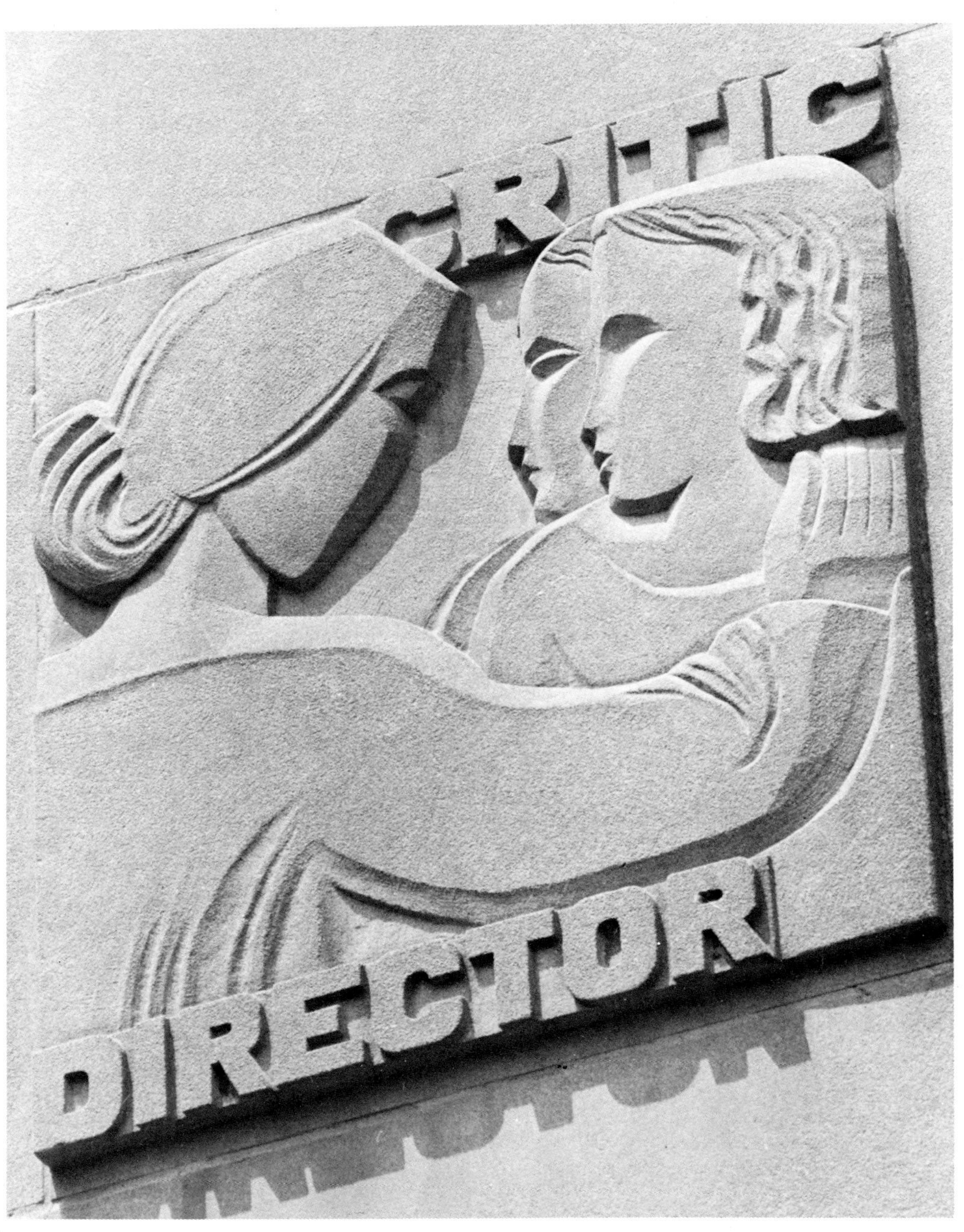
CRITIC
DIRECTOR

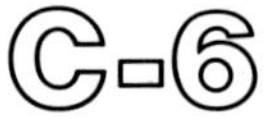

Douglas M. Gruizenga (1947-   )
UNTITLED

1972, concrete over steel and polystyrene, 8'9"

Paul V. Sangren Hall, Western Michigan University
N. Hays Drive, Kalamazoo

This sculpture was created by a graduate art student and is permanently located in a sculpture exhibition area outside of Sangren Hall at Western Michigan University. The tactile work is composed of geometric forms which are broken by voids and connected by angular forms. Many of the forms and voids are accentuated by the contrasting dark steel rods which outline them. The piece appears to be a giant machine that might slowly roll away from its location.

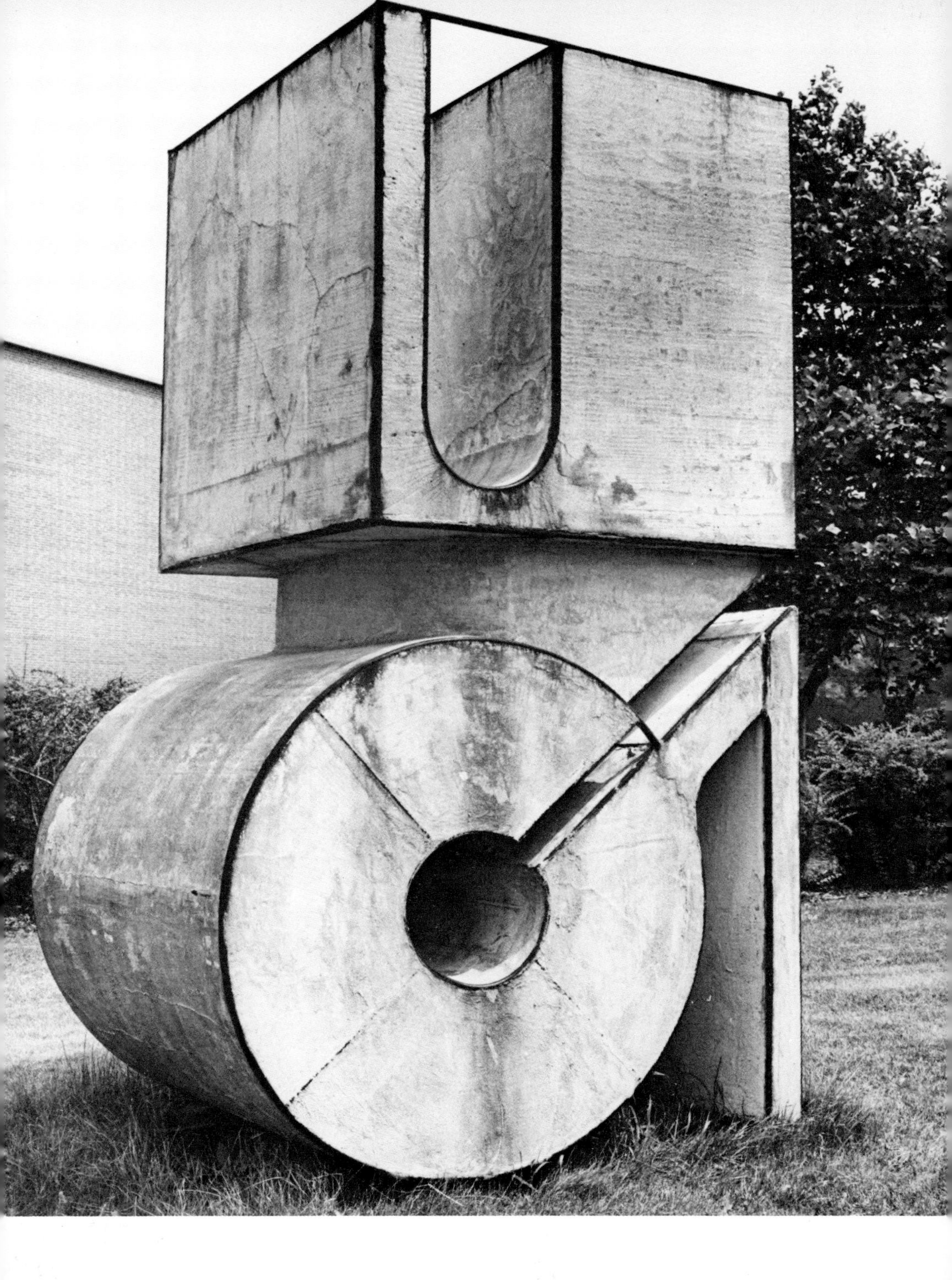

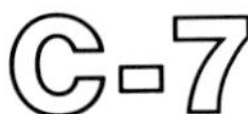

Carole Harrison (1933-   )
THREE FIGURES

1971-1972, brass, 12'2"

Fine Arts Plaza, Miller Auditorium,
Western Michigan University
Auditorium Road, Kalamazoo

This trinity, composed of a female surrounded by two males, was commissioned by President James Miller for the Fine Arts Plaza at Western Michigan University. Funds for the sculpture, which was dedicated on December 10, 1972, were provided by Mrs. Dorothy Upjohn Dalton. The textured figures bring a human presence to the plaza and interact with the horizontal and vertical lines of the surrounding architecture. Each individual figure is composed of fragmented forms, yet each flows and connects with the other. The figures and their spatial relationships reflect on the inner flow of emotions that shape the way in which people relate to each other.

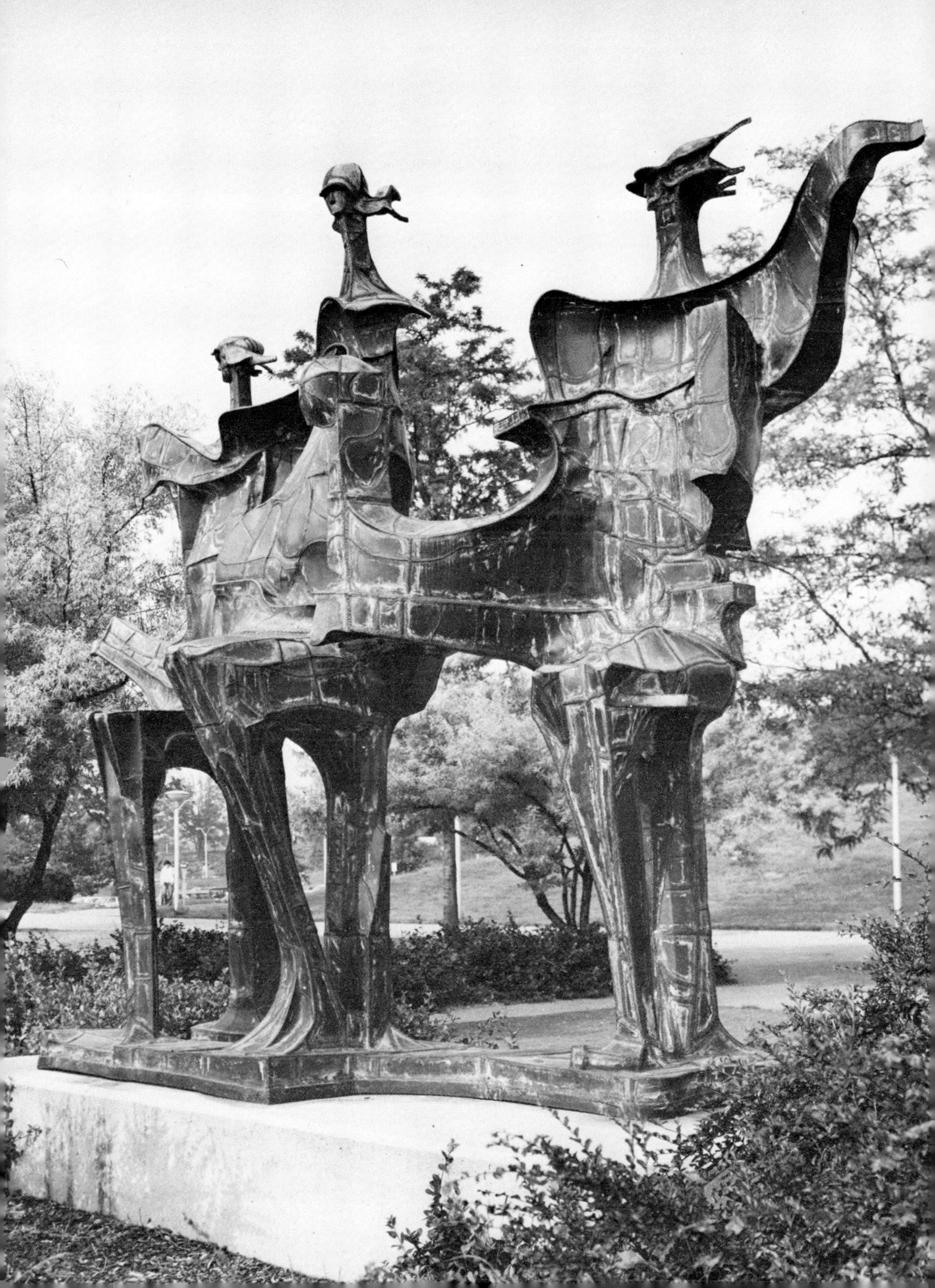

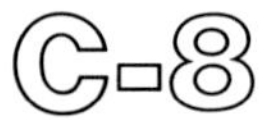 **Gerald C. Dumlao** (1935-   )
SUN DISC

1970, bronze, 5′

Shaw Theatre, Western Michigan University
W. Shaw Lane, Kalamazoo

Sun Disc was created through a cooperative effort at Western Michigan University to place original works of art on the campus. The university provided materials and services so that faculty member Gerald Dumlao could create this work. The sculpture was originally placed closer to Miller Auditorium, but was reworked and moved to its present location after it toppled from the original base. As the title suggests, the sculpture combines the motion of the wheel with the immobility of the disc, both ancient symbols of the sun. The work is oriented in an east-west direction which allows light to be reflected from the surfaces of the disc and to penetrate the mysterious openings in the center of the form. The piece suggests the cyclical, cosmic forces of life which have endured since the beginning of time. It also suggests that illumination comes from a divine centering which can penetrate the inner depths of each human being.

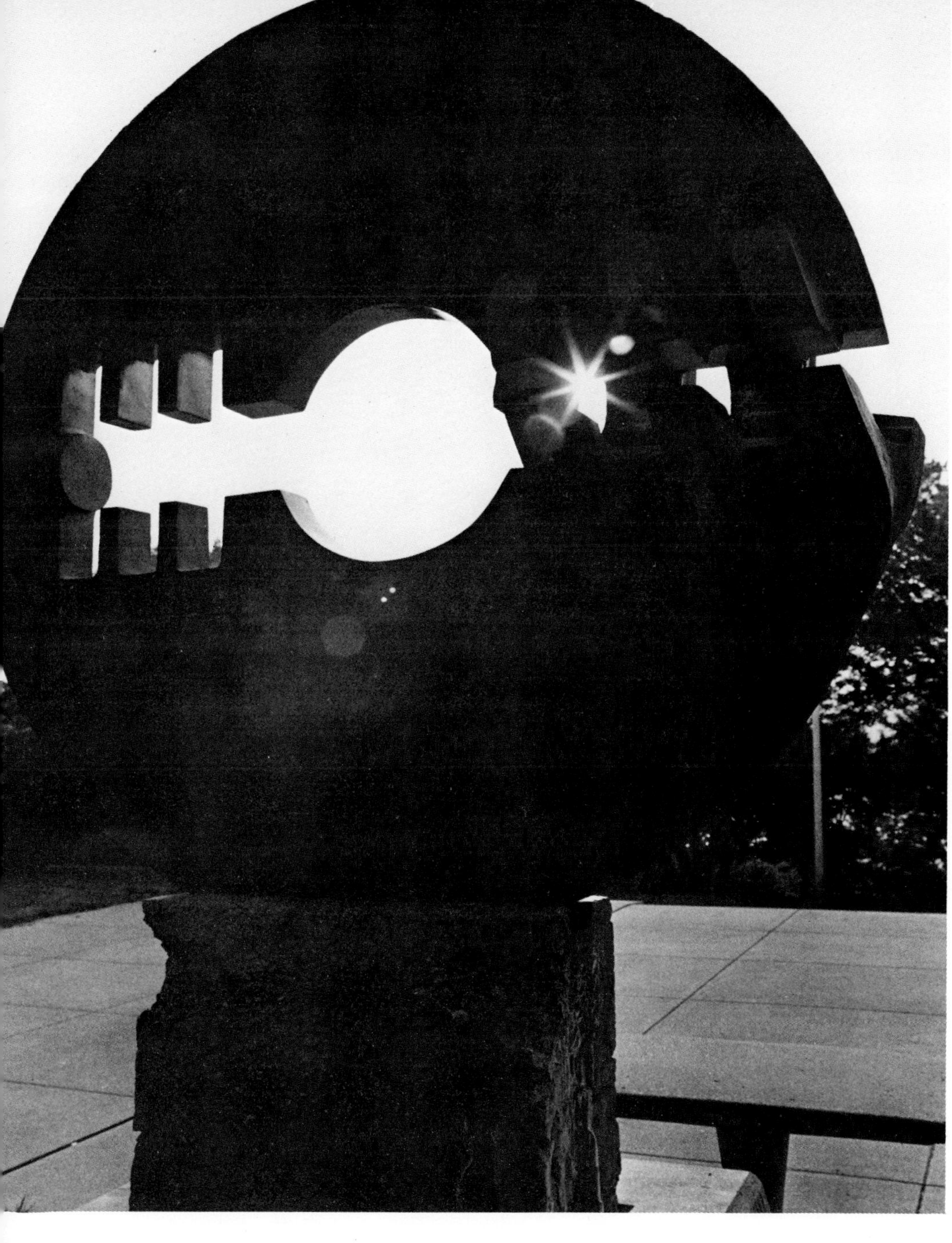

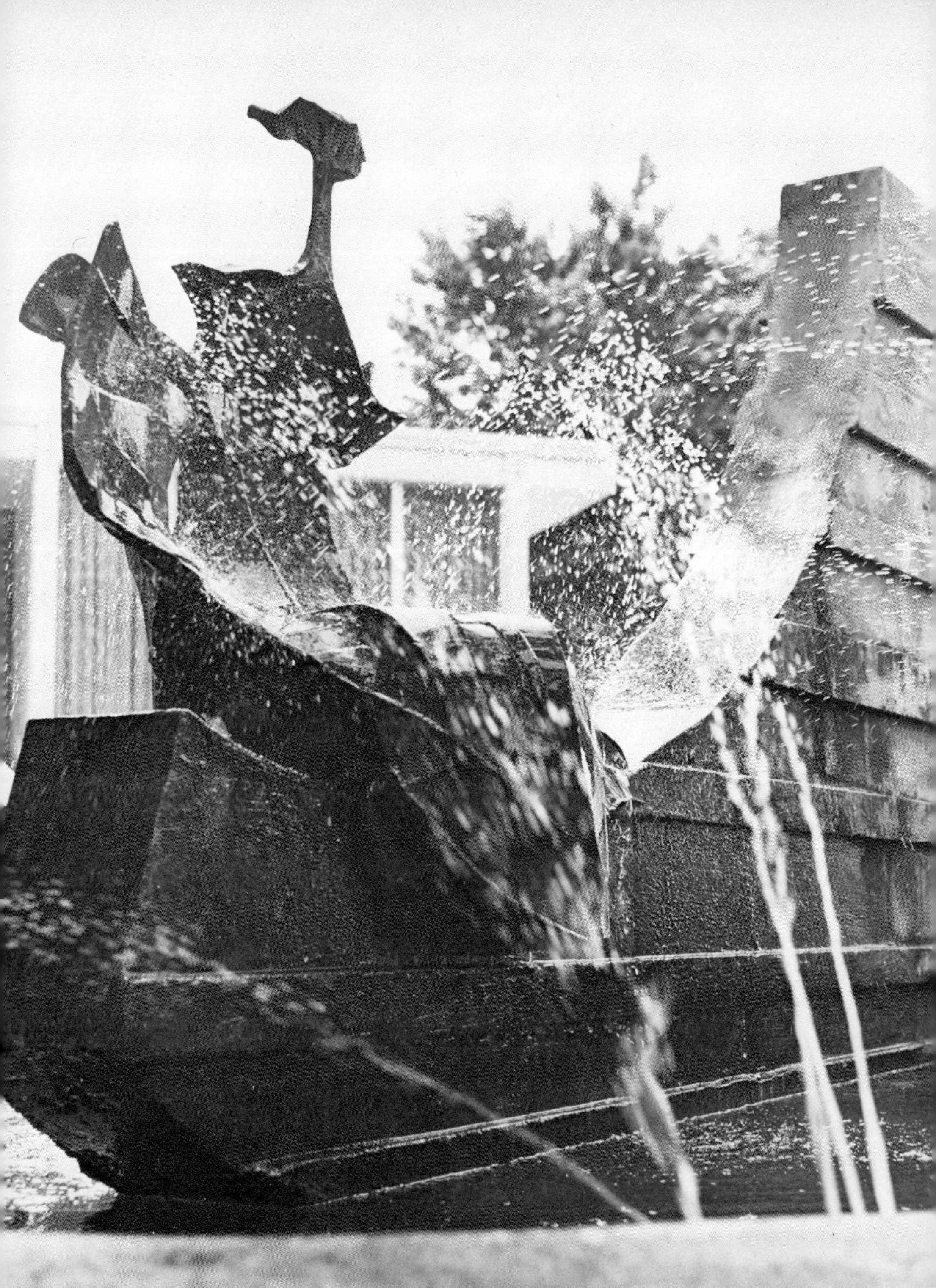

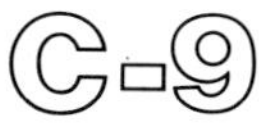

Carole Harrison (1933-   )
FOUNTAIN

1970, brass, 4'6"

Steinman-Dudley Company
1020 S. Westnedge, Kalamazoo

The fountain was commissioned by Robert Steinman
for the lawn of his real estate office. Composed of
welded, segmented forms which encourage the
collection of water on their broad surfaces, the figure
suggests the sensation of drifting through water. The
curved form upon which she sits helps to conjure up
the image of a mermaid or a figurehead on the prow
of a ship and adds to the watery image.

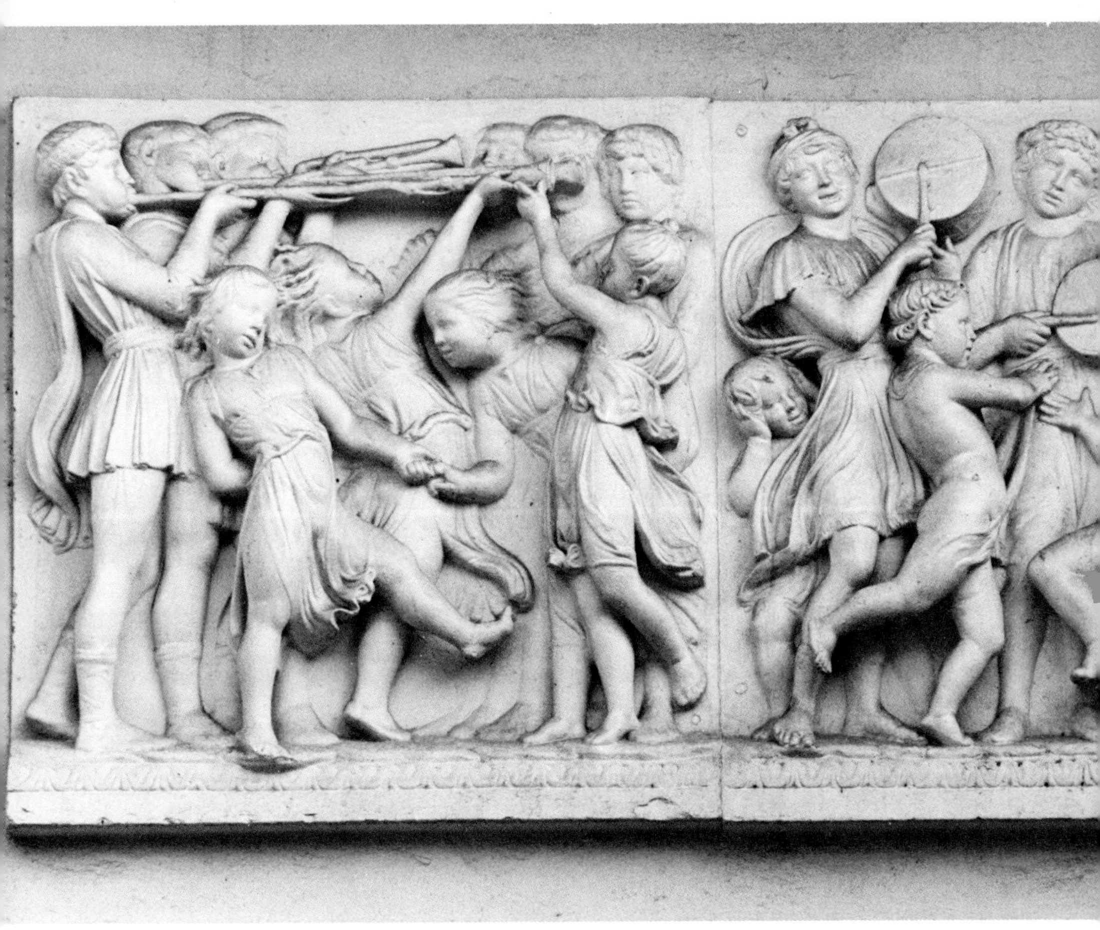

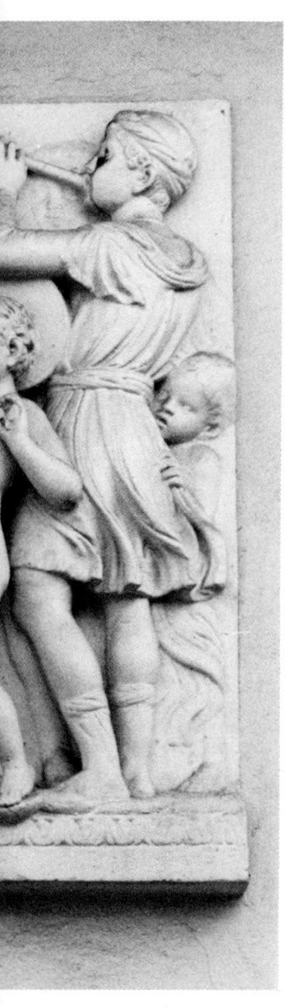

After Luca della Robbia (c. 1399-1482)

TRUMPETERS, DRUMMERS
from the CANTORIA

c. 1910, unknown material, c. 3'6"

Zelinger House
133 W. Vine Street, Kalamazoo

The reliefs over the door of the Zelinger House were taken from Luca della Robbia's *Cantoria* or singers' gallery which was commissioned for the Cathedral of Florence in 1431. This and a later companion gallery by Donatello (c. 1386-1466) were replaced with larger galleries to accommodate the singers and musicians for the marriage of Ferdinando de' Medici in 1688. The galleries eventually found their way to the cathedral museum where they are presently located. The marble *Cantoria* is Luca's earliest known work and reflects his sweet, restrained Renaissance style which is best known through his glazed blue and white terra cotta reliefs. The *Cantoria* contains ten relief panels illustrating the text of Psalm 150 which was sung at the end of the mass. The Psalm exhorts the worshipper to praise the Lord through music and dance. The Zelinger panels correspond to the left and right panels in the upper register of the *Cantoria* and portray the trumpeters and drummers dancing on heavenly clouds. The Zelinger reliefs and other *Cantoria* panels over the fireplace are thought to have been incorporated into the house by a former owner who was an opera singer.

C-10

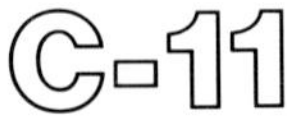

Artist Unknown
"BOY READING A BOOK"

c. 1927, copper, c. 12″

Washington Square Library
1244 Portage Street, Kalamazoo

On November 22, 1927, the Washington Square Library building was dedicated. Designed by Kalamazoo architects Billingham and Cobb, it was the first branch library to be constructed in Kalamazoo. In addition to serving as a weathervane, the young boy hunched over his book also points the way to education through reading books.

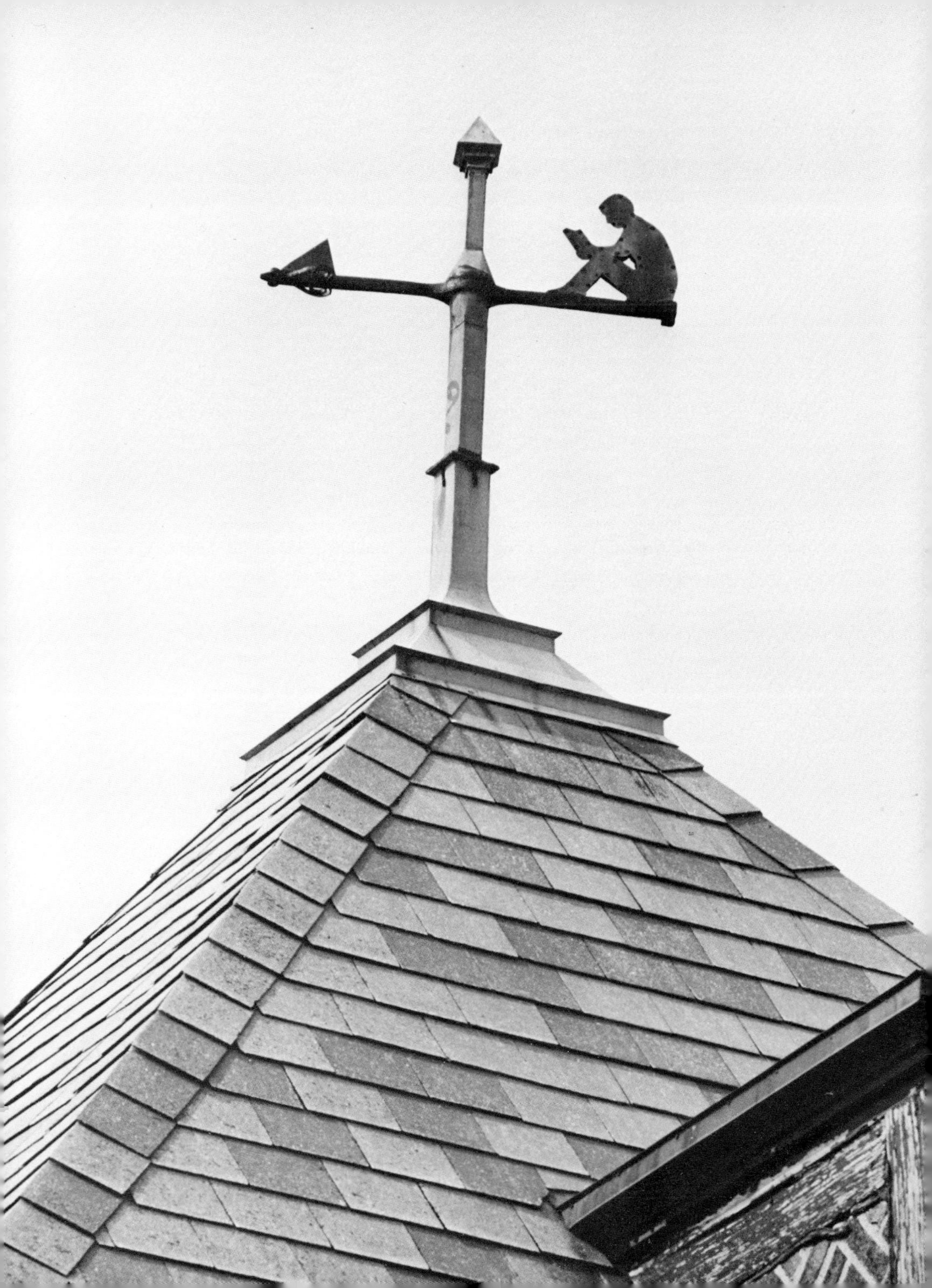

C-12 Bernhard Zuckermann (1912-   )
THE WADERS

1953, bronze, 5'10"

Mount Ever-Rest Memorial Park
3941 S. Westnedge Avenue, Kalamazoo

In May of 1955 two identical bronze fountains were
placed at the entrance to Mount Ever-Rest Memorial
Park. The sculptural group *The Waders* is composed of
three herons leisurely wading amongst cattails. The
model for the sculpture was created by Bernhard
Zuckermann in his studio in Carrara, Italy, and castings
were made in nearby Viareggio. The fountains have not
functioned since 1976 when the pools were converted
to flower beds. Zuckermann has also carved several
marble sculptures for the cemetery.

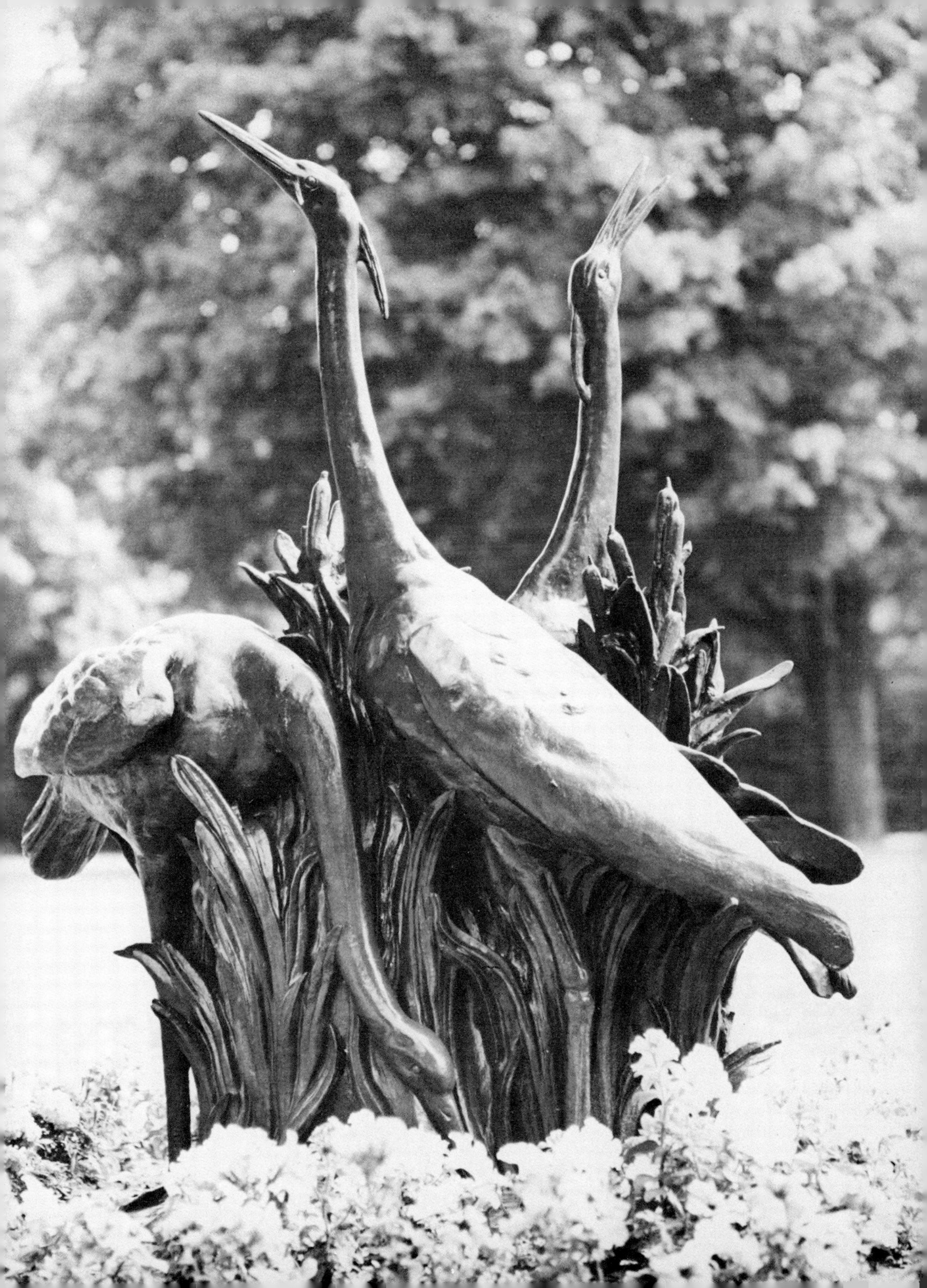

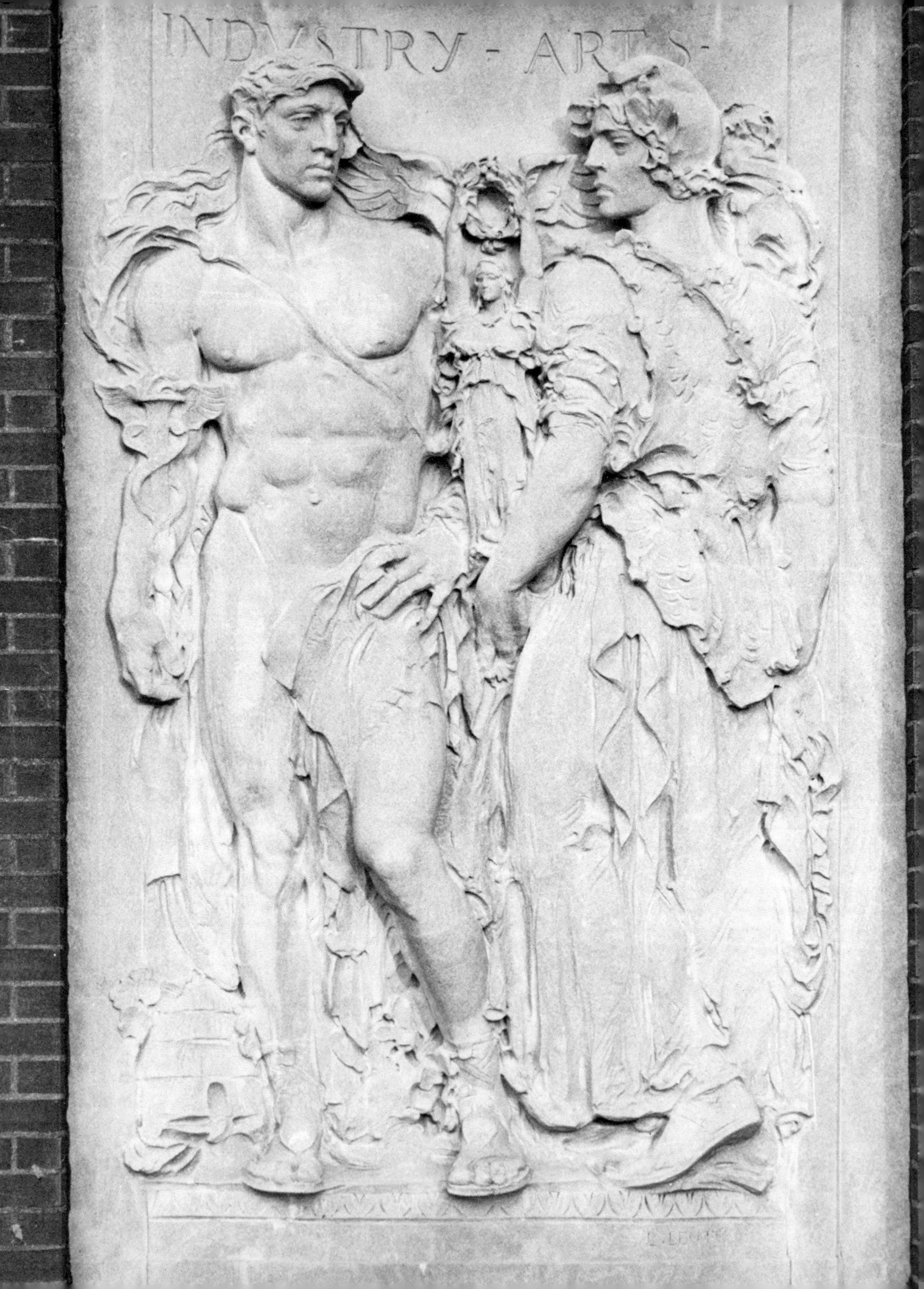

INDVSTRY · ARTS ·

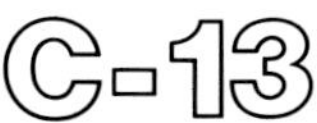

Leo Lentelli (1879-1961)

COMMERCE AGRICULTURE; INDUSTRY, ARTS

c. 1923, marble, 8'1"

[L. Lentelli]

Cathedral Church of Christ the King
2600 Vincent Avenue, Kalamazoo

These two panels of baroque sculptural reliefs, allegorically portraying *Commerce, Agriculture, Industry,* and the *Arts,* were commissioned for the entryway of the Straus Building in Chicago which was designed by the Chicago firm of Graham, Anderson, Probst, and White in 1923. In one panel (see p. iv) the classically draped figures represent *Commerce* holding a ship and *Agriculture* with a sheaf of wheat thrown over her shoulder and a jug of water at her feet. Between the two may be the youthful Mercury, god of commerce and travel, who holds a winged wheel symbolizing commerce. In the other panel (opposite) the robust figure of *Industry* holds the caduceus or staff of Mercury while at his feet is a beehive symbolizing industry. The figure representing the *Arts* holds a Nike, goddess of Victory, in her left hand, who is ready to reward creative human efforts with a crown of laurel leaves. The building was remodeled after it was purchased by Continental Companies in 1943 and the facade found its way to the Miller Monument Company in Elkhart, Indiana. There it was discovered in the early 1950s by William P. Favorite of Detroit while purchasing a monument for a cemetery plot in his hometown of Sturgis, Michigan. Favorite subsequently offered the reliefs to the Cathedral Church of Christ the King in 1968 through newly appointed Dean Benjamin V. Lavey, former rector of St. John's Episcopal Church in Sturgis. The reliefs were incorporated into the new building (see p. 94), designed by Irving R. Colburn and Associates of Chicago, as a reminder that the church's mission is "to minister to all of God's people and to all forces in society." The reliefs also serve as a reminder that the Cathedral is located between Detroit and Chicago on the old Territorial Road (I-94) which was a gateway to Chicago and the Midwest when it was laid out in 1830.

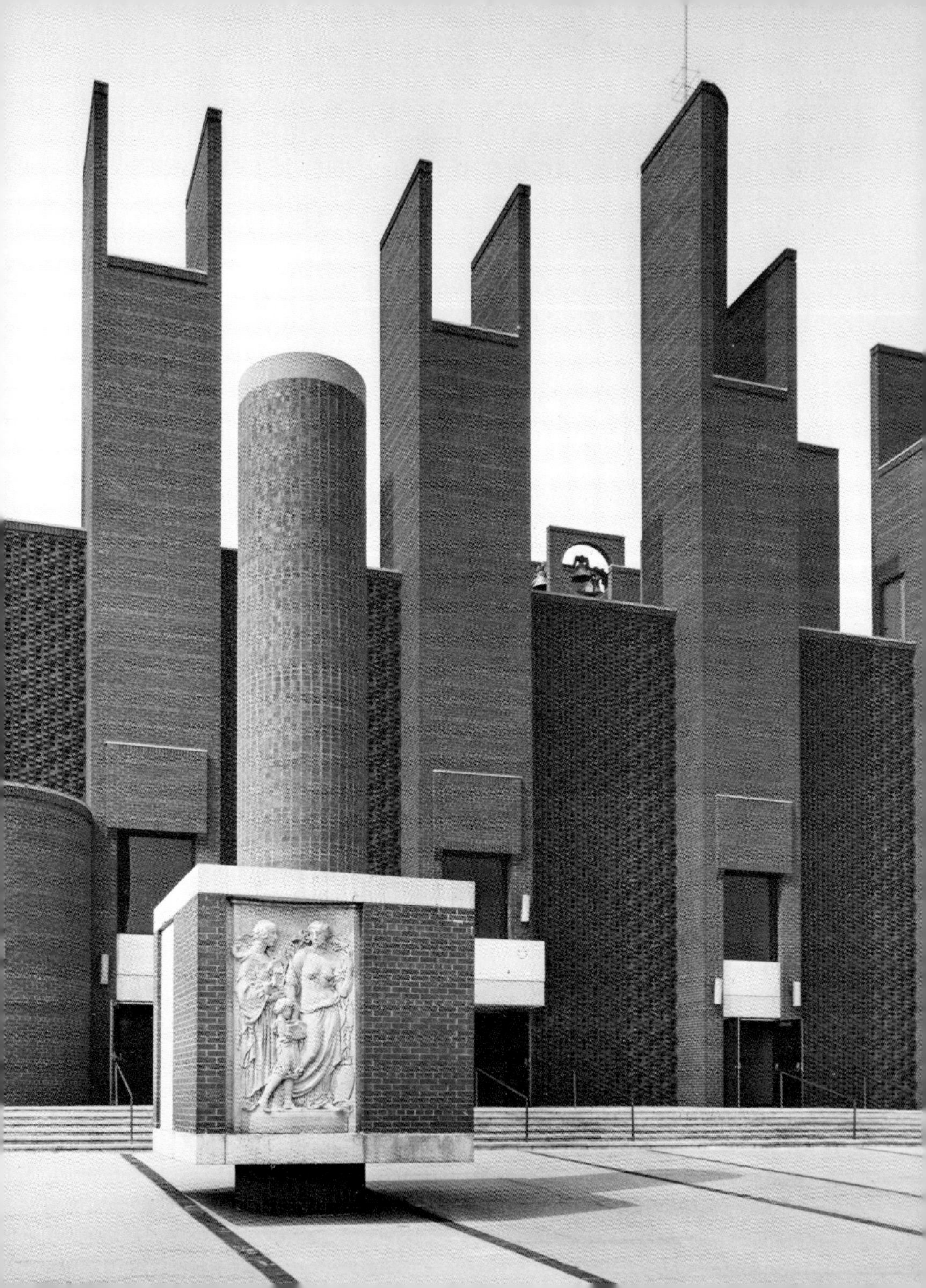

ARTISTS' BIOGRAPHIES

BARTHOLI
The monument to Bishop Borgess, Nazareth College, Kalamazoo, Michigan, c. 1903-1905, is considered the work of Bartholi. The attribution appeared in the following newspaper article: "Dedication of Monument Monday," *Kalamazoo Gazette,* 7 October 1906:5.

POMPEO L. COPPINI (1870-1957)
Born in Moglia, Italy, Coppini graduated from the Academy of Fine Arts in Florence in 1889. He came to New York in 1896 and later had studios in Chicago and San Antonio. In the latter city, he was head of the Fine Arts Department at Trinity University from 1943 to 1945 and founded the Coppini Academy of Fine Arts. His many commissions include *Richard B. Westnedge,* Kalamazoo, Michigan, 1900; *George Washington,* Mexico City, 1911; *James P. Clarke,* Statuary Hall, Washington, D. C., 1918; *General William Rufus Shafter,* Galesburg, Michigan, 1919; *John Ball Memorial,* Grand Rapids, Michigan, 1925; and the *Spirit of Sacrifice,* Alamo Heroes Cenotaph, San Antonio, Texas, 1936.

GERALD C. DUMLAO (1935-   )
Born in Portsmouth, Virginia, Dumlao received a B.F.A. from the Cleveland Institute of Arts in 1964 and an M.F.A. from Cranbrook Academy of Art, Bloomfield Hills, Michigan, in 1966. He taught at Western Michigan University, Kalamazoo, Michigan, from 1966 to 1976. He is currently teaching at San Diego State University. His works can be found at the Butler Institute of American Art, Youngstown, Ohio; the Cleveland Museum of Art; and the Michael C. Rockefeller Arts Center Gallery, State University of New York, Fredonia. His *Sun Disc* of 1970 is located at Western Michigan University, Kalamazoo, Michigan.

DOUGLAS M. GRUIZENGA (1947-   )

Gruizenga received a B.S. in 1970 and an M.A. in 1972 from Western Michigan University. After graduation, he worked for six months as an industrial clay modeler at Chrysler Corporation. His works include an untitled piece, Sangren Hall, Western Michigan University, Kalamazoo, Michigan, 1972; *Industrial Forms I*, South Bend, Indiana, 1974; and *Industrial Forms II*, Kalamazoo, Michigan, 1974-1975.

CAROLE HARRISON (1933-   )

Born in Chicago, Harrison received a B.F.A. in 1955 and an M.F.A. in 1956 from the Cranbrook Academy of Art, Bloomfield Hills, Michigan. She attended the Central School of Arts and Crafts in London, England, on a Fulbright Scholarship in 1957. In that year she was also awarded a Huntington Hartford Fellowship and in 1960 she received an award from the Louis Comfort Tiffany Foundation. She taught at Western Michigan University, Kalamazoo, Michigan from 1960 to 1974 and has taught at the State University of New York, Fredonia, since 1975. Her many works include *Guard,* Holland High School, Holland, Michigan, 1965; a sculptural group for the Oak Park Library, Oak Park, Illinois, 1966; *Seated Female,* Kalamazoo Institute of Arts, 1969; *Fountain,* Steinman-Dudley Company, Kalamazoo, Michigan, 1970; and *Three Figures,* Western Michigan University, Kalamazoo, Michigan, 1972.

ALFONSO IANNELLI (1888-1965)

Born in Andretta, Italy, Iannelli came to Newark, New Jersey, in 1898. At the age of thirteen he became an apprentice in a jewelry factory and shortly thereafter began studying at the Newark Technical School under William St. John Harper (1851-1910). When he was seventeen, he attended the Art Students League in New York where he studied with George B. Bridgman (1864-1943) and Gutzon Borglum (1867-1941). He worked briefly in the latter's studio before opening his own studio. In 1908 he left New York for Cincinnati where he was a designer for a lithography company. By 1910 he was working in Los Angeles and from there he was called to Chicago around 1913 to work with Frank Lloyd Wright (1869-1959) on the Midway Gardens (1913-1914). He returned to California briefly before settling permanently in Chicago. He taught at the Los Angeles Institute of Arts from 1911 to 1913, the Chicago Academy of Fine Arts from 1923 to 1924, and at the Chicago Art Institute from 1928 to 1930 where he was Head of the Department of Design. His numerous works include the design of the Packard automobile, 1915; sculptural reliefs, Woodbury County Courthouse, Sioux City, Iowa, 1916; *Fountain of the Pioneers*, Bronson Park, Kalamazoo, Michigan, 1939; reliefs for St. Francis Xavier Church, Kansas City, Missouri, 1940; and *Rock of Gibralter*, Prudential Building, Chicago, Illinois, c. 1950.

JERALD W. JACKARD (JACQUARD) (1937-   )
Born in Lansing, Michigan, Jackard studied sculpture at Michigan State University where he received a B.A. in 1960 and M.A. in 1962. After graduation he taught at the Kalamazoo Institute of Arts until 1966, with 1963 spent studying bronze casting in Florence under a Fulbright Scholarship. From 1966 until 1975 he taught at the University of Illinois, Chicago Circle Campus, and is currently teaching at Indiana University. He received a Guggenheim Fellowship in 1972. Jackard's works include an untitled sculpture at Kresge Art Center Gallery, Michigan State University, East Lansing, Michigan, 1965; *Silent Defender*, a purchase prize of the Detroit Institute of Arts in 1965; the *Passing of Colored Volume*, Kalamazoo Institute of Arts, Kalamazoo, Michigan, 1968; and a commissioned work for the Chicago Transit Authority, 1974.

JAMES G. JACKSON III (1940-   )
Born in Muskegon Heights, Jackson studied metallurgy at Ferris
State College, Big Rapids, Michigan, from 1958 to 1959. He also
studied at Muskegon Junior College from 1962 to 1963, where he
received an associate degree, and at Western Michigan University,
Kalamazoo, Michigan. His works in Kalamazoo include *Growing
Together*, Helen Coover Center, 1976; untitled sculpture, Fisher-
Graff Steel Corporation, 1976; *Black Madonna*, Black Nationalist
Church, 1977; and *Twenty Eight Degrees*, Gordon P. Rogers,
Architect, 1978.

CHARLES KECK (1874-1951)
Born in New York City, Keck studied at the National Academy of
Design, the Art Students League, and with Augustus Saint-
Gaudens (1848-1907) from 1893 to 1898. He also studied with
Philip Martiny (1858-1927) and at the American Academy in
Rome from 1901 to 1905. His numerous works include Soldiers'
Memorial, Pittsburgh, Pennsylvania, c. 1905; U.S.S. *Maine*
Memorial Relief Tablet, one casting in Bronson Park, Kalamazoo,
and another in Galesburg, Michigan, 1913; *Booker T. Washington*,
Tuskegee, Alabama, 1922; *Amicitia*, Rio de Janeiro, Brazil, c. 1921;
Governor Alfred E. Smith, New York, c. 1950.

THEODORE ALICE RUGGLES KITSON (1871-1932)
Born in Brookline, Massachusetts, Kitson studied in Paris with
Pascal Adolphe Jean Dagnan-Bouveret (1852-1929). She received
honorable mention at both the Paris Exposition in 1889 and the
Paris Salon of 1890, the latter award being the first ever given to
an American woman. She also studied with the American sculptor
Henry Hudson Kitson (1865-1947) whom she married in 1893.
She executed many public sculptures which are located
throughout the United States, including *Kosciusko*, Boston,
Massachusetts; *Victory*, Hingham, Massachusetts; the *Volunteer of
'61*, Newburyport, Massachusetts, 1902; eight portrait medallions
for the General Sherman Monument, Washington, D.C., 1903;
The Hiker, Minneapolis, Minnesota. Approximately fifty castings

have been made of the latter, including three in Michigan, in the cities of Grand Rapids (c. 1927), Kalamazoo (c. 1923), and Lansing, (c. 1945). The last *Hiker* was erected in Washington, D.C. in 1964.

ALOIS LANG (1872-1954)

Lang was born in Oberammergau, Bavaria, a village famous for woodcarving and the production of a Passion Play, and was apprenticed to his cousin Andrea Lang when he was around fourteen years old. He came to the United States about 1890 and worked for several firms, including Irving and Cass of Boston. He returned to Europe around 1898 and came back to Boston in 1901. In 1903 he became an employee of the American Seating Company in Manitowac, Wisconsin, and moved to Grand Rapids, Michigan, when the firm transferred operations in 1927. His carvings can be found throughout the United States and include those located at Christ Church, Cranbrook, Bloomfield Hills, Michigan; Shrine of the Little Flower, Royal Oak, Michigan; Christ Church, Boston; University of Chicago Chapel, Chicago; and All Saints Church, Pasadena, California. He may have carved the wooden tympanum for the First Presbyterian Church, Kalamazoo, Michigan, c. 1930.

LEO LENTELLI (1879-1961)

Born in Bologna, Italy, Lentelli studied in Bologna and Rome before coming to the United States in 1903. He was an assistant in the studio of several New York sculptors including A. Stirling Calder (1870-1945) and Philip Martiny (1858-1927). He taught at the California School of Fine Arts in San Francisco and the Art Students League in New York. His many works include figures for the reredos of the Cathedral of Saint John the Divine, New York; five figures for the San Francisco Public Library, c. 1916; *Apollo and the Muse,* Steinway Building, New York; *Commerce, Agriculture, Industry, Arts,* Straus Building, Chicago, c. 1923, now located at the Cathedral Church of Christ the King, Kalamazoo, Michigan; *Faun,* Boca Raton Club, Florida, 1931; and *James Cardinal Gibbons,* Washington, D.C., 1932.

DWAYNE LOWDER (1936-   )

Born in Albemarle, North Carolina, Lowder received a B.A. in 1959 and an M.A. in 1963 from The University of North Carolina. A painter, designer, and sculptor, Lowder was on the staff of the Kalamazoo Institute of Arts from 1963 to 1965. He taught at The University of North Carolina from 1962 to 1963 and has been teaching at Western Michigan University, Kalamazoo, Michigan, since 1966. In addition to the untitled sculpture, Kalamazoo Institute of Arts, Kalamazoo, Michigan, 1969, his works can be found in the North Carolina Museum of Art, Raleigh; the Mint Museum of Art, Charlotte, North Carolina; the Bundy Art Gallery, Waitsfield, Vermont; and Western Michigan University, Kalamazoo, Michigan.

KIRK NEWMAN (1926-   )

Born in Dallas, Texas, Newman received a B.A. in 1949 and an M.A. in 1951 from the University of Tulsa. He also studied at the University of Iowa in 1949 and at the Ruskin School, Oxford University, Oxford, England, in 1975. He taught at the Extension Division, University of Michigan, from 1949 to 1956; the University of Tulsa in 1951; and at Kalamazoo College from 1957 to 1958. He has taught at the Kalamazoo Institute of Arts since 1956. A painter, printmaker, and sculptor, Newman's sculpture in Kalamazoo includes *One,* People's Church, 1971; *People,* Kalamazoo Institute of Arts, 1973-1974; and *When Justice and Mercy Prevail, Children May Safely Play,* 1976. Newman's works can also be found in many collections including the Earl Ludkin Collection, Chicago; Syracuse University, Syracuse, New York; Numazu, Japan; and Portaroz, Yugoslavia.

BERNARD S. PALCHICK (1945-   )

Born in Chicago, Illinois, Palchick received a B.A. from Purdue University in 1967 and an M.F.A. in 1971 from the Rhode Island School of Design. He taught at the latter school from 1971 to 1972 and has been teaching at Kalamazoo College, Kalamazoo, Michigan, since 1972. In addition to *Détente,* Kalamazoo College, 1973, his work is represented in several private collections.

CORRADO JOSEPH PARDUCCI (1900-   )
Born in Pisa, Italy, Parducci came to New York in 1904 and
graduated from P.S. 95 in 1915. He was introduced to
architectural modeling when he began working for Donnelly and
Ricci and served an apprenticeship with Ricci and Zari from 1917
to 1921. While in New York he studied at the Beaux Art Institute
of Design and with George Bridgman (1864-1943) at the Art
Students League. After the apprenticeship, he was employed by
Anthony di Lorenzo who sent him to Detroit in 1924. Parducci
stayed on and opened his own studio in 1925. His numerous
commissions can be found throughout the United States. Among
his Detroit area works are the Bear Fountain at the Zoo, the Buhl,
Fisher, and Guardian buildings, Meadowbrook Hall, and the Music
Hall Theater. His Lansing works can be found on the First Baptist
Church, Pilgrim Congregational Church, Grace Lutheran Church,
St. Paul's Episcopal Church, Lansing Avenue Pumping Station,
Lansing Public Library, Michigan Bell Telephone Company, and
Sexton High School. His works can also be found on the
Kalamazoo County Building, Kalamazoo, Michigan, and the
Grand Rapids Civic Auditorium and Michigan National Bank
Building (Grand Rapids Trust), Grand Rapids, Michigan.

GEORGE RICKEY (1907-   )
Born in South Bend, Indiana, Rickey moved to Scotland with his
family in 1913. He attended Trinity College, Glenalmond,
Scotland from 1921 to 1926 and received a B.A. in 1929 and an
M.A. in 1941 from Balliol College, Oxford, England. He also
studied at the Ruskin School, Oxford, 1928-1929; Academie Lhote
and Academie Moderne, Paris, 1929-1930; Institute of Fine Arts,
New York University, 1945-1946; the University of Iowa, 1947;
and the Chicago Institute of Design, 1948-1949. A painter,
sculptor, and author, Rickey has taught at many schools. They
include Artist-in-Residence, Olivet College, Olivet, Michigan,
1937-1939; Kalamazoo College and Kalamazoo Institute of Arts
(he also served as Director for the latter), Kalamazoo, Michigan,
1939-1940; Knox College, Galesburg, Illinois; Muhlenberg

STUDIO OF ARCHITECTURAL SCULPTURE
This firm was selected by the City Commission to prepare the
sculpture models for the new City Hall in Kalamazoo, Michigan,
on December 8, 1930.

BERNHARD ZUCKERMANN (1912-   )
Born in New York, Zuckermann has studios in both New York
and Carrara, Italy, the latter having been in the Zuckermann
family for three generations. Zuckermann studied in New York at
Columbia University, the National Academy of Design, and the
Beaux Arts Institute and at the Academy of Fine Arts in Florence,
Italy. His sculpture at Mount Ever-Rest Memorial Park,
Kalamazoo, Michigan includes *The Waders*, 1953; *Last Supper*, c. 1960;
Suffer the Little Children, c. 1963; *Christ Stilling the Waters*, c. 1962;
Christus, c. 1963; and *Resurrection*, c. 1970. Among his other works
are the Kennedy Memorial Fountain, University of Tampa,
Tampa, Florida; *Christopher Columbus*, City Hall, Elizabeth, New
Jersey; and *Sermon on the Mount*, Manila, Philippines.

SELECT BIBLIOGRAPHY

Andrus, Percy H. "Historical Markers and Memorials in Michigan."
Michigan History Magazine 15 (Spring 1931): 167-374.

Armstrong, Tom, et al. *200 Years of American Art*. [Boston]:
David R. Godine in association with the Whitney Museum,
1976.

Burroughs, Clyde H. "Painting and Sculpture in Michigan."
Michigan History Magazine 20 (Autumn 1936): 395-409 and
21 (Spring 1937): 39-54, 141-157.

Craven, Wayne. *Sculpture in America*. New York: Crowell, 1968.

Doezma, Marianne and Hargrove, June. *The Public Monument and
Its Audience*. Cleveland: The Cleveland Museum of Art, 1977.

Durant, Samuel W. *History of Kalamazoo County, Michigan*.
Philadelphia: Everts & Abbott, 1880.

Ekdahl, Janis. *American Sculpture*. Art and Architecture Information
Guide Series, vol. 5. Detroit: Gale Research Co., 1977.

Friedlander, Lee. *The American Monument*. New York: The Eakins
Press Foundation, 1976.

Gibson, Arthur Hopkin (comp.). *Artists of Early Michigan*. Detroit:
Wayne State University Press, 1975.

Goode, James M. *The Outdoor Sculpture of Washington, D.C.*
Washington, D.C.: Smithsonian Institution Press, 1974.

Gregerson, Charles E. "Early Adler & Sullivan Work in Kalamazoo."
Prairie School Review 11 (Third Quarter 1974): 5-15.

Griggs, Joseph. "Alfonso Iannelli, the Prairie Spirit in Sculpture."
Prairie School Review 2 (Fourth Quarter 1965): 5-23.

Iannelli, Alfonso. "Kalamazoo's Fountain of the Pioneers."
American City 56 (September 1941): 50-52.

May, George S. (comp.). *Michigan Civil War Monuments*. Lansing:
Civil War Centennial Observance Commission, 1965.

Praus, Alexis A. (comp.). *Historical Markers and Memorials in Kalamazoo
and Kalamazoo County*. Kalamazoo: The Kalamazoo Historical
Commission, 1969.

Proske, Beatrice Gilman. *Brookgreen Gardens Sculpture.* New ed., rev.
and enl. Brookgreen, South Carolina: Brookgreen Gardens,
1968.

Rebori, A. N. "The Straus Building, Chicago." *Architectural Record*
57 (May 1925): 385-394.

Robinette, Margaret A. *Outdoor Sculpture, Object and Environment.*
New York: Watson-Guptill Publications, 1976.

Sculpture of a City: Philadelphia's Treasures in Bronze and Stone.
New York: Walker Publishing Co., Inc., 1974.

Sheridan, Leo J. and Clark, W. C. "The Straus Building, Chicago."
Architectural Forum 42 (April 1925): 225-228.

Taft, Lorado, *The History of American Sculpture.* New ed. with a
supplementary chapter by Adeline Adams. New York:
The Macmillan Co., 1930.

NOTE

While the above have been helpful, much of the documentary
material was collected in bits and pieces from a variety of sources
including local and state libraries, archives, museums, interviews, and
a field inventory. Source materials include an inventory form with
bibliography and photograph for each sculpture; local, county and
state histories; newspaper and magazine articles; correspondence;
photographs; and dedication booklets. All of the documentation will
be housed in the Michigan State University Archives and Historical
Collections, East Lansing, Michigan.

INDEX

Adler & Sullivan, Chicago, 6, 48

Angel, First Presbyterian Church (Lang ?), 3,36,37

Angels, Chapel, Mountain Home Cemetery (Artist Unknown), 5, 68, 69

Bardeen, Virginia Pratt, 31

Bartholi, 54, 55, 95

Billingham, M.J.C., Kalamazoo, 25

Billingham and Cobb, Kalamazoo, 88

Bishop Borgess (Bartholi ?), 5, 54, 55, 57, 95

Black, Frank D., 3

Black Madonna (Jackson), 62, 63, 98

Black Madonna, Shrine of the, 63

Black Nationalist Church, 63

Borgess, Bishop Casper H., 5, 54, 57, 95

"Boy Reading a Book" (Artist Unknown), 7, 88, 89

Bronson Park, 1, 2, 4, 5, 6, 9, 17, 18, 20, 22

Bronson, Titus, 1, 17, 25

Cantoria (Luca della Robbia), 87

Cathedral Church of Christ the King, 6, 7, 93, 94

Chressanthis, James, 10

City Hall Reliefs (Studio of Architectural Sculpture), 2, 3, 7, 38, 39, 102

Clark, Anna D., 43

Colburn, Irving R. and Associates, Chicago, 93

Commerce, Agriculture; Industry, Arts (Lentelli), iv, 6, 7, 92, 93, 94, 99

Coppini, Pompeo L., 3, 5, 60, 61, 64, 65, 95

Dalton, Mrs. Dorothy Upjohn, 10, 27, 28, 35, 80

DeSeille, Father Louis J., 74

Desenberg Building, 4, 6, 48

Détente (Palchick), 9, 72, 73, 100

Dumlao, Gerald C., 10, 82, 83, 95

Dunbar, Colonel G. Edwin, 5

Eberson, John, 6

Favorite, William P., 93

First Congregational Church, 3

First Presbyterian Church, 3, 36

Folz, Samuel, 46

Fountain (Harrison), 84, 85, 96

Fountain of the Pioneers (Iannelli), 2, 3, 7, 16, 17, 97

Four Lines Oblique Gyratory, Variation IV (Rickey), 9, 30, 31, 102

Galesburg, 3, 6, 65

Gargoyle, Ladies Library Association (Artist Unknown), 4, 42

Gargoyles and reliefs, First Congregational Church (Karompay), 3

Gay, Henry L., Chicago, 42

General Services Administration, Art-in-Architecture Program, 9

Gougler, Marcelline, 17

Graham, Anderson, Probst and White, Chicago, 93

Gruizenga, Douglas M., 9, 10, 50, 51, 78, 79, 96

Guardian Angel (Artist Unknown), 4, 56, 57

Harrison, Carole, 9, 10, 28, 29, 80, 81, 84, 85, 96, back cover

Henry Vandercook Hall Reliefs (Artist Unknown), 7

Hiker, The (Kitson), 2, 6, 22, 23, 98, 99

Hope, McCortie Monument, Mountain Home Cemetery (Artist Unknown), 5, 70, 71

Iannelli, Alfonso, 2, 3, 7, 16, 17, 96, 97

Industrial Forms II (Gruizenga), 9, 10, 50, 51, 96

Intermodal Transportation Center, 10

Jackard, Jerald, W., front cover, 9, 32, 33, 97

Jackson, James G. III, 62, 63, 98

Kahn, Albert, Detroit, 45

Kalamazoo Arts Council, 10

Kalamazoo College, 9, 72

Kalamazoo County Building Reliefs (Parducci), 3, 7, 8, 24, 25, 101

Kalamazoo Gazette Building Reliefs (Artist Unknown), 7, 44, 45

Kalamazoo Institute of Arts, 9, 10, 27, 28, 31, 33, 35

Kalamazoo Public Museum, 3

Kalamazoo State Hospital, 10

Karompay, George, 3

Keck, Charles, 2, 20, 21, 64, 65, 98

Kitson, Theodore Alice Ruggles, 2, 22, 23, 98

Klauder, Charles Z., Philadelphia, 36

Knecht, F. W., 10

Knecht, McCarty and Thebaud, Grand Rapids, 10
Ladies Library Association, 4, 42
Lang, Alois, 3, 36, 37, 99
Lavey, Dean Benjamin V., 93
Lavinia Spindler Hall Reliefs (Artist Unknown), 7, 76, 77
Lawrence, William, S., 3, 41
LeFevre Institute, 57, 74
Lentelli, Leo, iv, 6, 7, 92, 93, 94, 99
Lowder, Dwayne, xi, 9, 10, 26, 27, 100
Luca della Robbia. *See* Robbia, Luca della
McColl Memorial Fountain, 2, 17
McCortie, Amanda M. Wayne, 70
McCortie Monument, Mountain Home Cemetery, 5, 70, 71
McCortie, William H., 70
Mackie and Ellis Jewelers, 46
Maine, U.S.S., Memorial Tablet. *See* U.S.S. *Maine* Memorial Tablet
Malcomson, Calder and Hammond, Detroit, 76
Mall, Kalamazoo, 9, 46, 50
Michigan Council for the Arts, 9
Mount Ever-Rest Memorial Park, 8, 90
Mountain Home Cemetery, 4, 5, 68, 70
Myer, Charles, 9
National Endowment for the Arts, 9
Nazareth College, 4, 9, 54, 57
Newman, Kirk, 2, 5, 6, 9, 10, 18, 19, 34, 35, 100
O'Brien, Father Frank, 54
Palchick, Bernard S., 9, 72, 73, 100
Parducci, Corrado Joseph, 3, 7, 8, 24, 25, 101
Park Club Door Reliefs (Artist Unknown), 3, 4, 40, 41
Passing of Colored Volume (Jackard), front cover, 9, 32, 33, 97
People (Newman), 5, 9, 10, 34, 35, 100
Pickering, T. F., 46
Pratt, Evlyn Hall, 31
Public Works Administration (PWA), 8, 25
Rese, Bishop Frederic, 57
Richardson, Stephen H., 1
Rickey, George, 9, 30, 31, 101, 102
Road Piece (Chressanthis), 10
Riverside Cemetery, 59, 60

Robbia, Luca della, 7, 86, 87
Saint Augustine (Artist Unnown), 4, 74, 75
Saint Augustine Church, 4, 54, 57, 74
Schau-Powell Sport Centre Reliefs (Artist Unknown), 4, 48, 49
Seated Female (Harrison), 9, 28, 29, 96
Seth Thomas Clock (Artist Unknown), 4, 9, 46, 47
Shafter, General William Rufus (Coppini), 3, 5, 6, 20, 64, 65, 95
Smith, Hinchman & Grylls, Detroit, 25
Soldiers' Monument (Artist Unknown), 5, 6, 58, 59
Spindler, Lavinia, 76
State Theatre Reliefs (Artist Unknown), 6
Steinman-Dudley Company, 85
Stone, Mrs. Lucinda H., 42
Straus Building, Chicago, 6, 93
Studio of Architectural Sculpture, 2, 3, 39, 102
Sullivan, Louis, 48
Sun Disc (Dumlao), 10, 82, 83, 95
Super Summer, 10
Talbot, Dennis, 74
Three Figures (Harrison), 10, 80, 81, 96, back cover
Urban renewal, 9
U.S.S. *Maine* Memorial Tablet (Keck), 2, 6, 20, 21, 64, 65
Waders, The (Zuckermann), 90, 91, 102
Wallace, Leon E., 42, 43
Washington Square Library, 7, 88
Weary and Alford, Chicago, 39
Western Michigan University, 7, 8, 9, 10, 76, 78, 80, 82
Westnedge Avenue, 60
Westnedge, Colonel Joseph B., 60
Westnedge, Mrs. Mary B., 60
Westnedge, Richard B. (Coppini), 5, 6, 60, 61, 95
When Justice and Mercy Prevail, Children May Safely Play, (Newman), 2, 6, 9, 10, 18, 19, 100
Work Projects Administration (WPA), 8, 76
Works Progress Administration (WPA), 8, 17
Wright, Frank Lloyd, 17
Zelinger House, 7, 87
Zuckermann, Bernhard, 8, 90, 91, 102

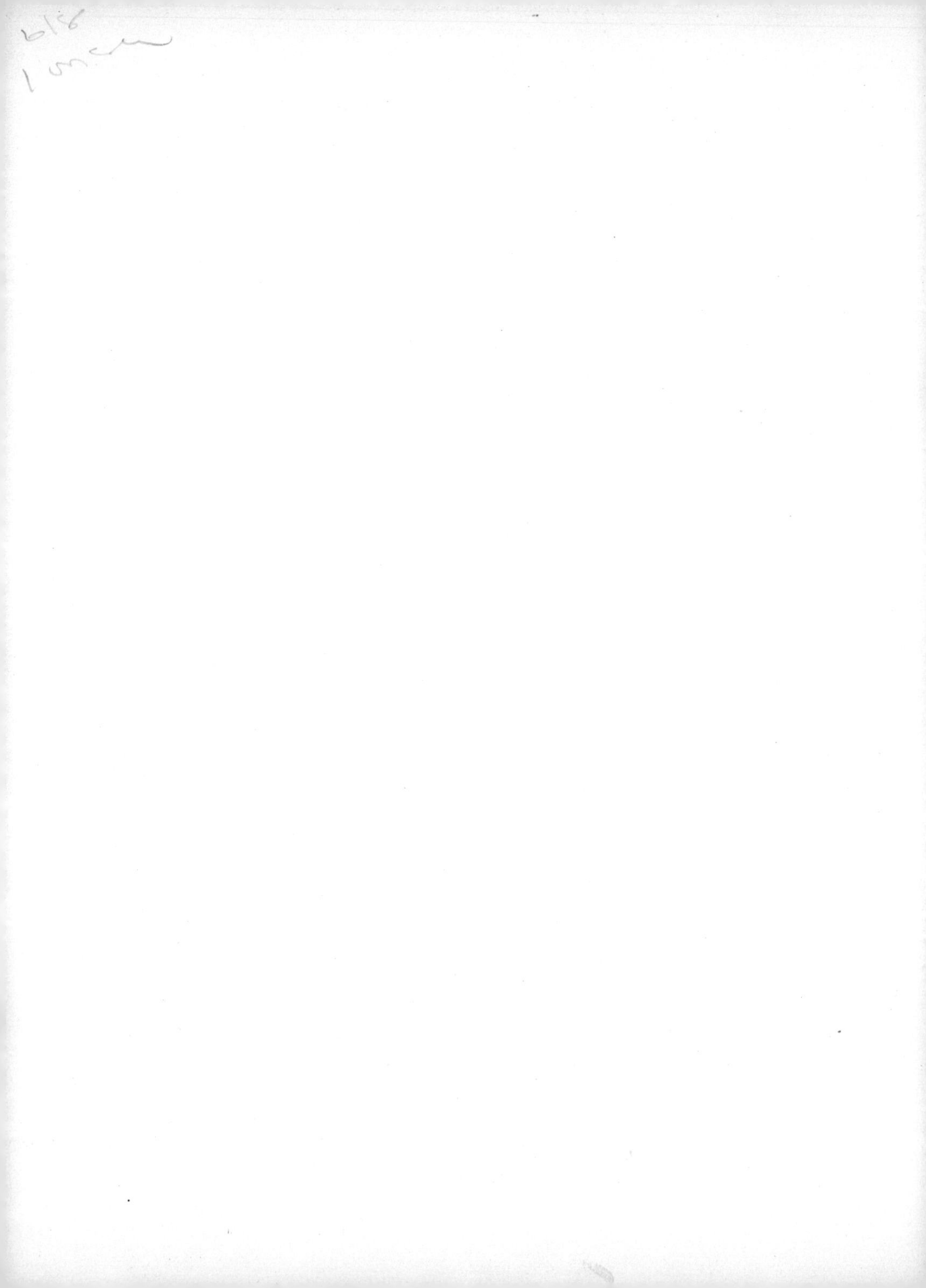